Oct 2016

I
Best Wishes
Vicki [signature]

Books by Vicki Rickabaugh
With photography by Pamela Turner

Spirits United:
The Sacred Connection, 2010

Gateway to the Universe:
Knowing Your Inner Self, 2010

In the Beauty of the Sunset:
A Spiritual Journey, 2011

Books by Vicki Rickabaugh & Veronica Grace
With illustrations by Vincent Gagliardi, Jr.

The Mysteries of Veron:
The Ruby Realm, 2010

The Mysteries of Veron:
The Carnelian Realm, 2011

Gateway to the Universe
Knowing Your Inner Self

Vicki Rickabaugh

Photographs by Pamela Turner

Published by Interwoven Connections
Howell, NJ, USA

Copyright © 2010 by Vicki Rickabaugh and Pamela Turner

All rights reserved. No part of this publication may be reproduced, distributed or transmitted in any form or by any electronic or mechanical means, or stored in a database or retrieval system, without the prior written permission of the publisher, except by a reviewer who may quote brief passages in a review.

First Printing, 2010
Second Printing, 2011

Published by
Interwoven Connections
PO Box 686
Howell, NJ 07731
www.interwovenconnectionspubs.com

ISBN-13: 978-0-9829582-0-9

Dedication

For my Guardian Angel who has given me belief,
inner tranquility, stillness and strength.

Even though I will only know your spirit for the moment,
the merging of the spirits will be forever.

Fatima, I dedicate this book to you,
the extraordinary being who has shown me
the glowing light within today and tomorrow.
This is the beauty of the moment with all its grace and glory.

Acknowledgements

With my husband Rick, love allows our hearts to embrace
all the seasons of life with joy, happiness, and trust.
To see and feel the colors of the universe
is truly love; it is an awakening.

My children and grandchildren—Gloria, George, Peggy, Marc,
Jenny, Kirsten, Ashley, Michael, Nicole and Mya—
You will walk down many paths in your lives.
Wherever the journey takes you,
know that you will always be loved.
Your spirit is within me
and my spirit will always be a part of you.

I honor my mother, Marilyn:
the depth of my gratitude is like the universe,
it is immeasurable.

For Pam, my spirit sister,
In the reflection of you, I have seen myself,
and that has changed my life forever.

With all the kindness and compassion that embraces
who you are, Iris, thank you for the journey.

To Bubbles and Joe: The giving or receiving of a gift
cannot compare to the knowing of the true gift itself.
You are gentle souls who softly touch many.

I could not have found my way and continued on this
path alone. I would like to thank those who have walked
along with me, giving of themselves and
adding their uniquely individual colors to my life:
Lee and Warren, Margaret, Syd,
Ellie FGM and Hugh, Nicole and Joel, Leslie and Dan,
Shell and Sharon, Linda and Nelson, Judy
Nancy, Larry, Steven, JoAnne, Katherine,
Karl, Barbara and Joe, Linnea, Kem,
Sara, Gina, Ken, Liz and Chrissy,
Stephanie, Jessica, Paula and David, Joyce,
Hannelore, Sherry, Alyson, and Mary.

Who am I?

I am the knowing, greater than thoughts,
emotions, or senses that emanate from
within the human body and mind.

I am more than words that are spoken or
that can be defined. I am the spirit within
the gentle winds that softly touches a
soul then quietly soars away
through the boundless heavens.

I am the We, the One.

What is the purpose of my existence?

It is to give without expectation,
to love unconditionally,
to share life's sacred spirit
with kindness, understanding,
and compassion.

Honoring All.

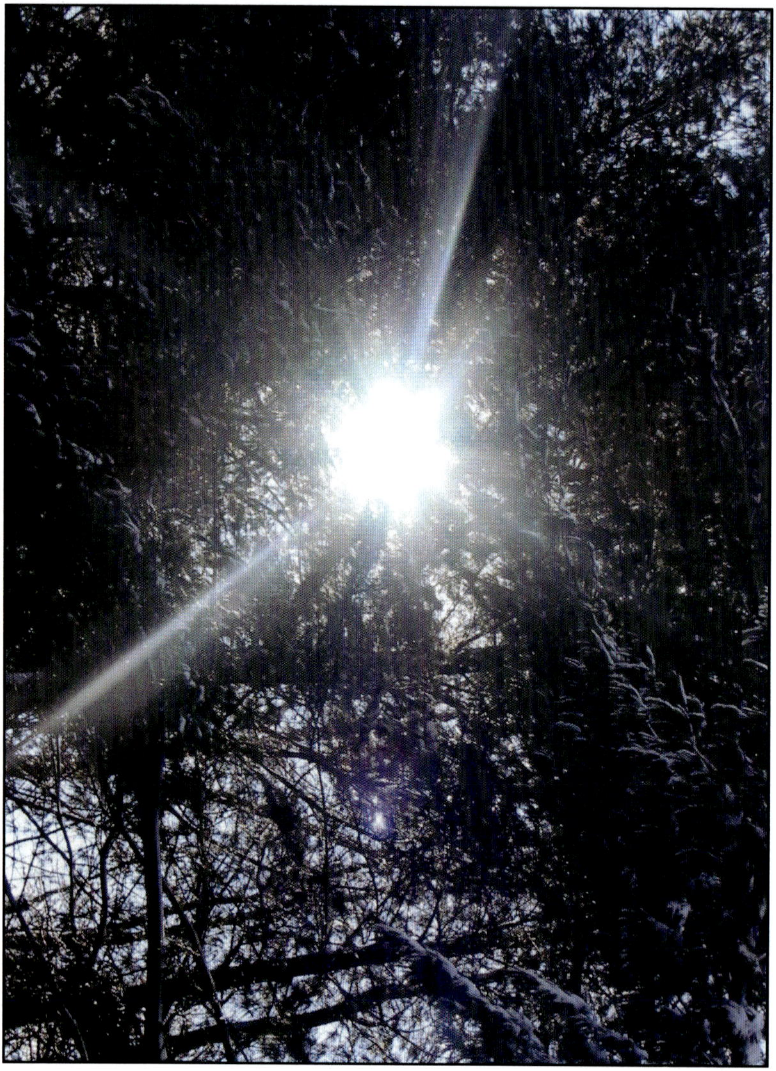

The messenger of light came and gently
touched me with her spirit,
embracing me with kindness,
Compassion, and trust.

The power of love was seen and known.

This is the sacred connection
throughout the universe.

This is the spirit and the message.

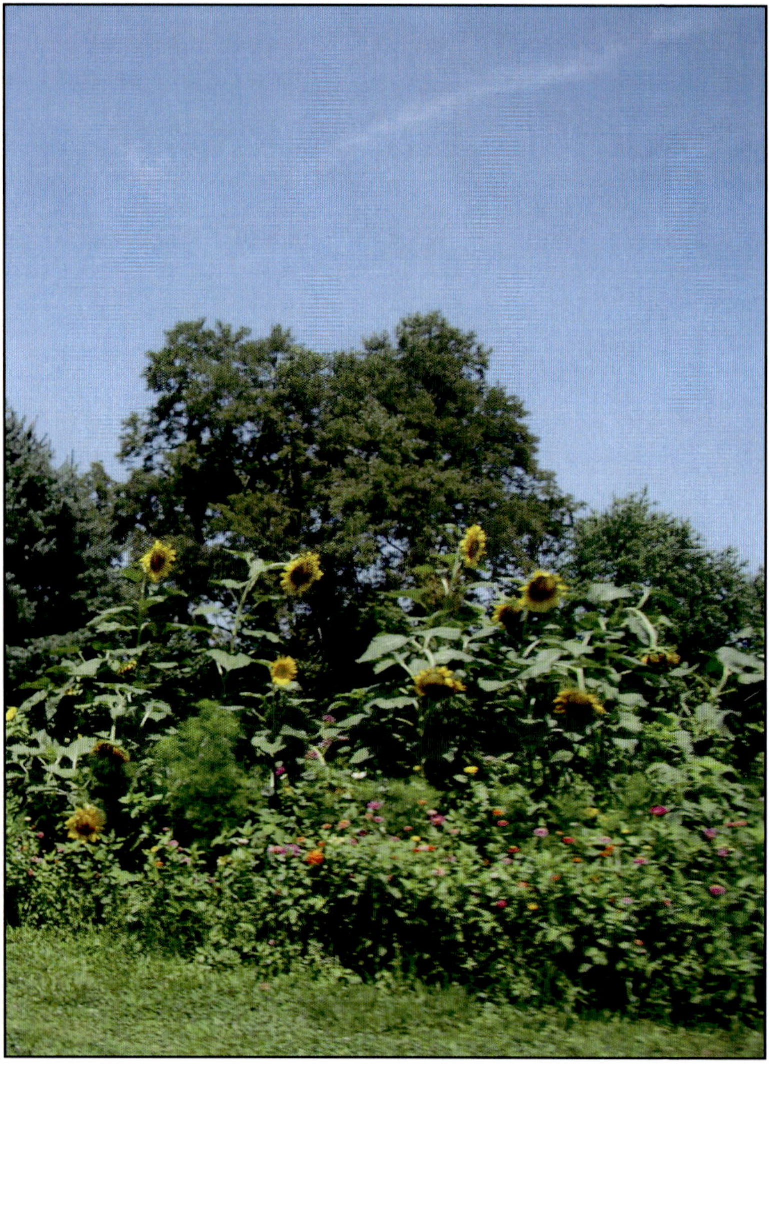

If every fertile mind
could reap that of which you have planted,
there would be a harvest of kindness and love.
The spirit of peace, happiness, and joy
would fill the universe.

Each one of us in our heart and soul,
has beauty and goodness,
but sometimes the inner soul
gets locked within the vault of space,
with the combination lost.

Fear not, it is not lost forever.

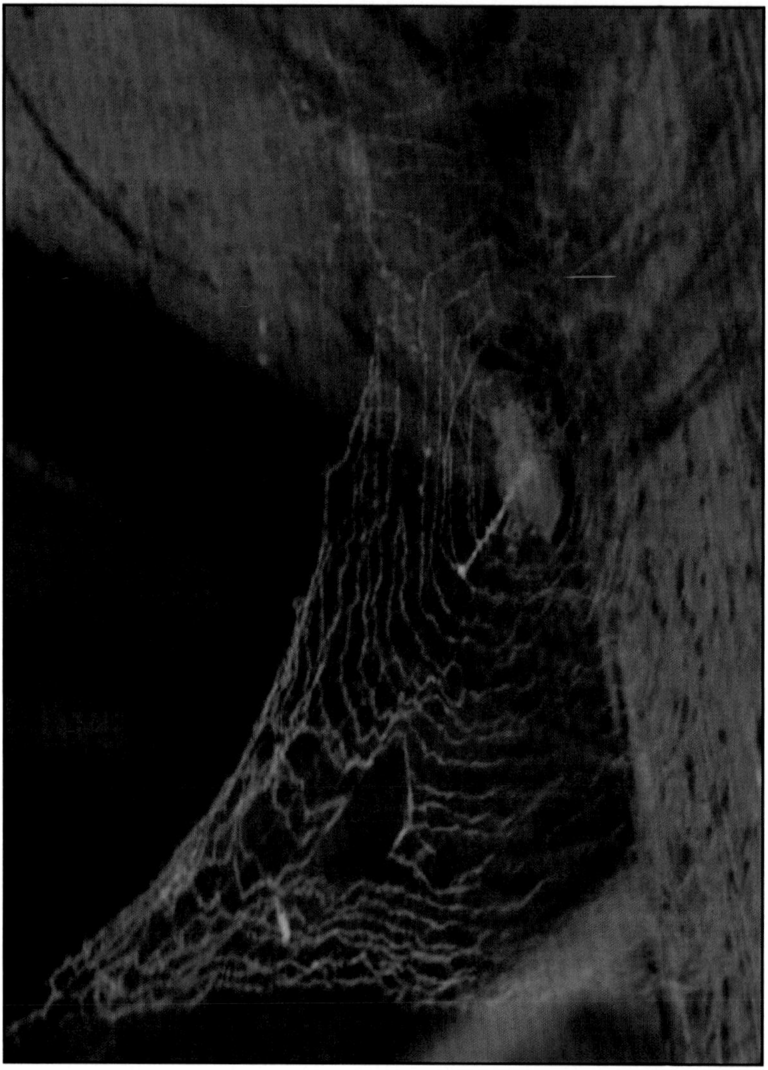

The divine matrix, the web, connects everything
in the universe to everything else.

This web spreads strand by strand,
yet is all part of the one.

At the same time, just as important,
each strand is separate and unique.

It is the distance between the space
of the other strands that makes it
individual and private unto itself;

Individual and private but part of the whole.

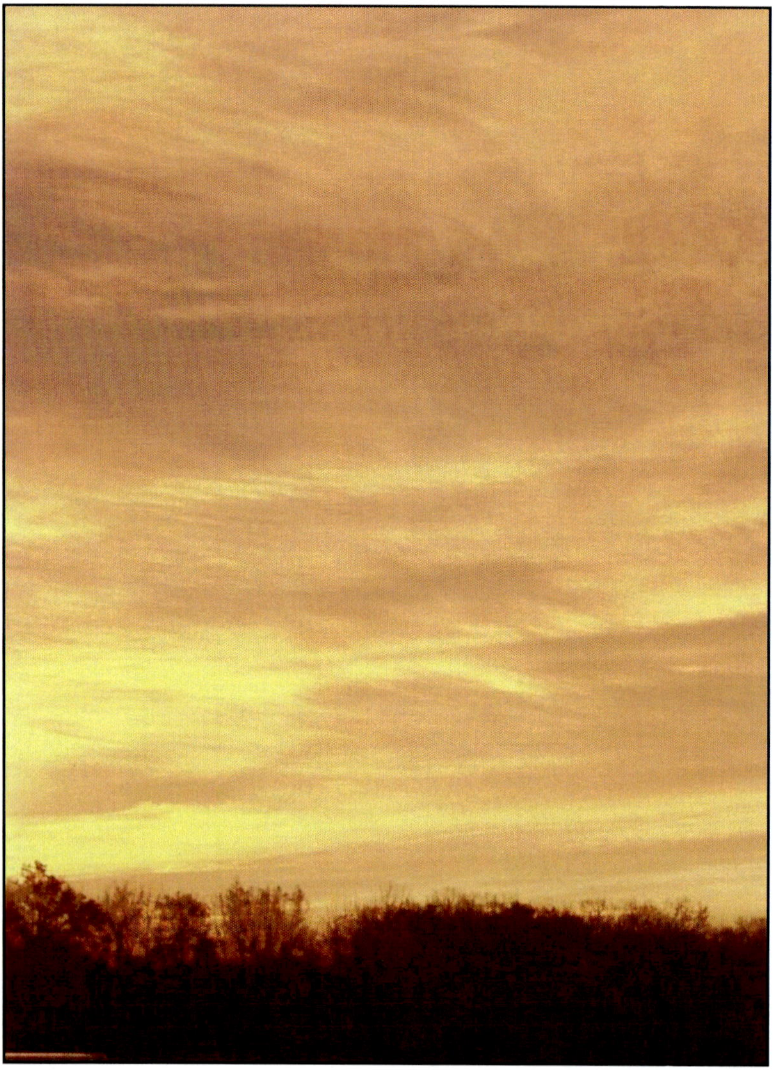

A happy heart greets the new morn
and sees that all things are possible.

Believe that the universal spirit is seen
and known by you and what you give.

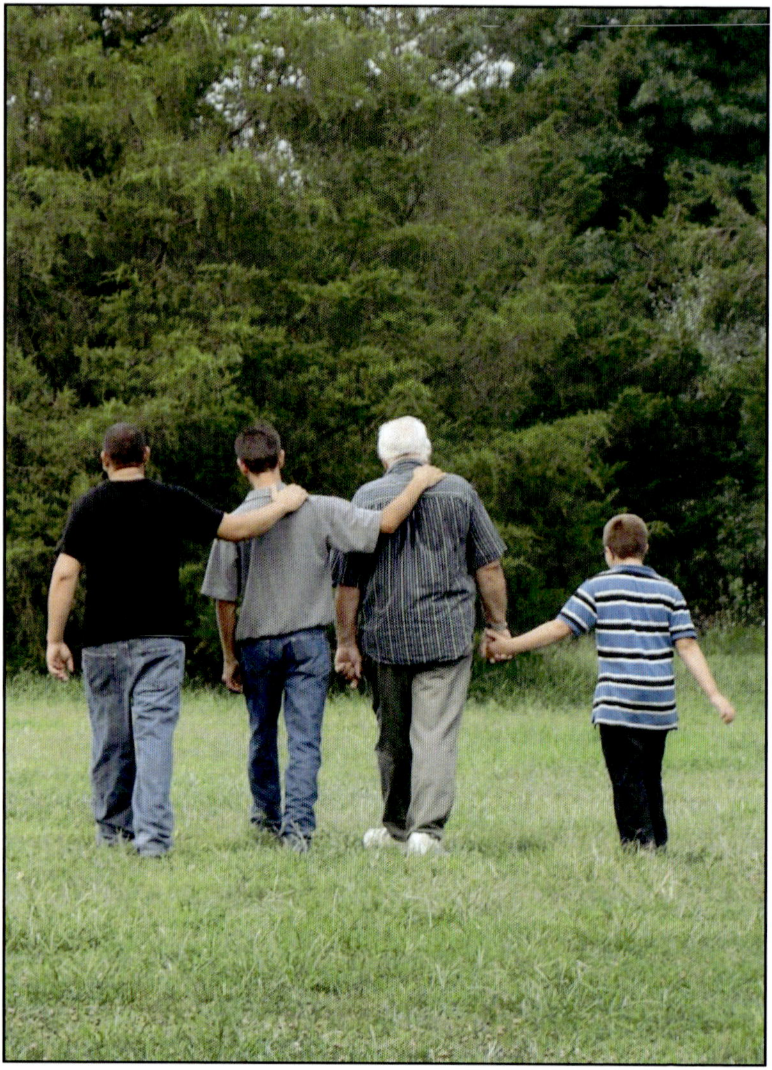

Sometimes I wonder
how many times have I met you
on my journey?

I wonder what we were like,
and then I smile.

It does not matter.

I know what we are today,
and I am blessed.

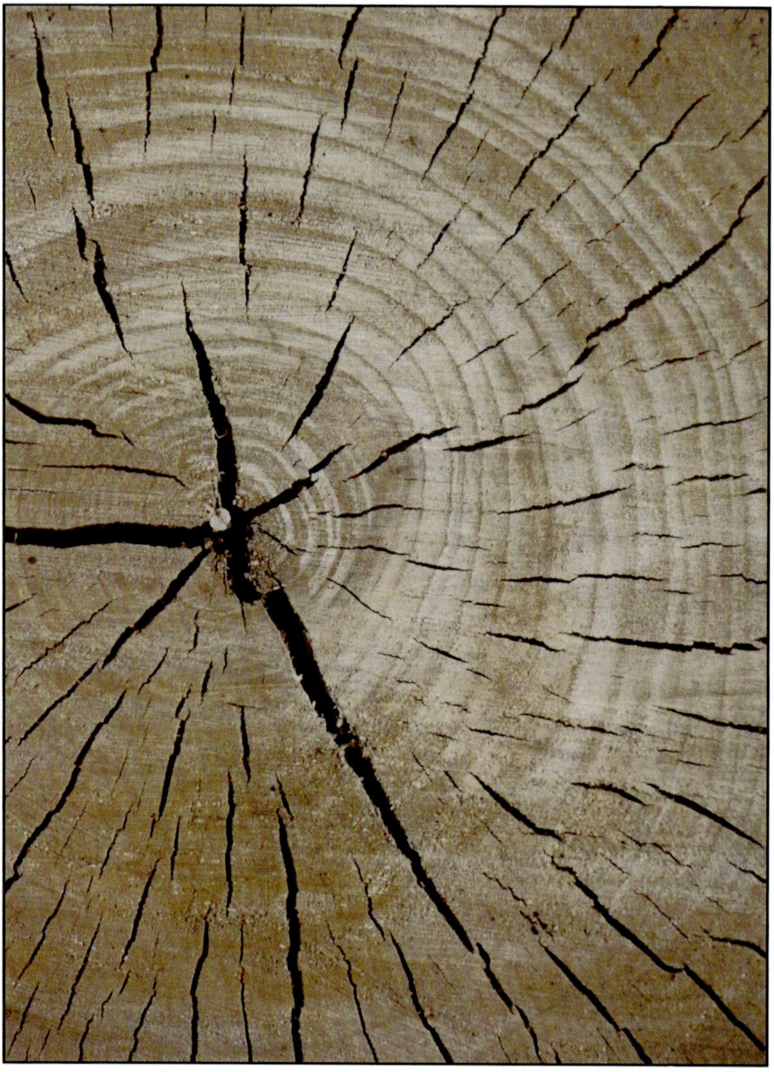

The world will someday know that we are all connected; one energy, many vibrations within the one knower.

What was lost through the generations will then be found.

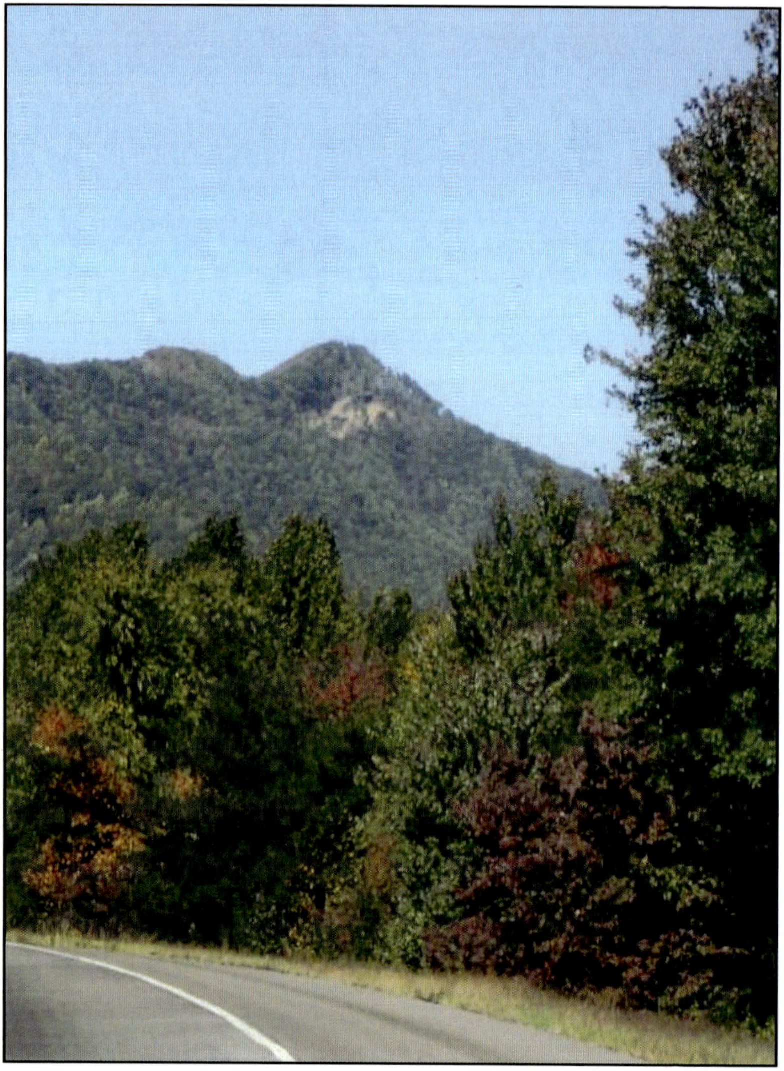

We live in a physical world.

But beyond our physical senses,
beyond this physical realm,
is a portal where visions can be seen
and all is connected.

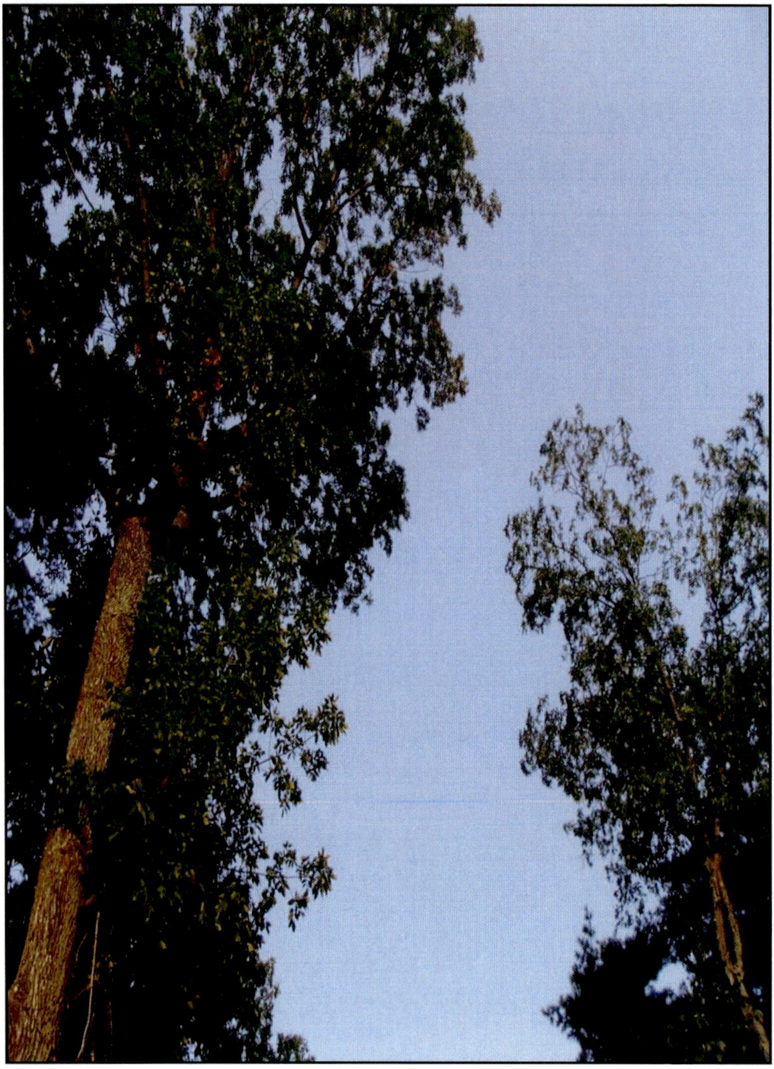

Each one of us creates our own boundaries
within the body, mind, and spirit.
We can stay trapped,
imprisoned in these boundaries,
accepting their limitations,
or we can realize that the only limits
in life are the ones we place on ourselves

Soar boundlessly,
knowing the sky is infinite
and so are we.
That is where all life is.
There is where you can find me.

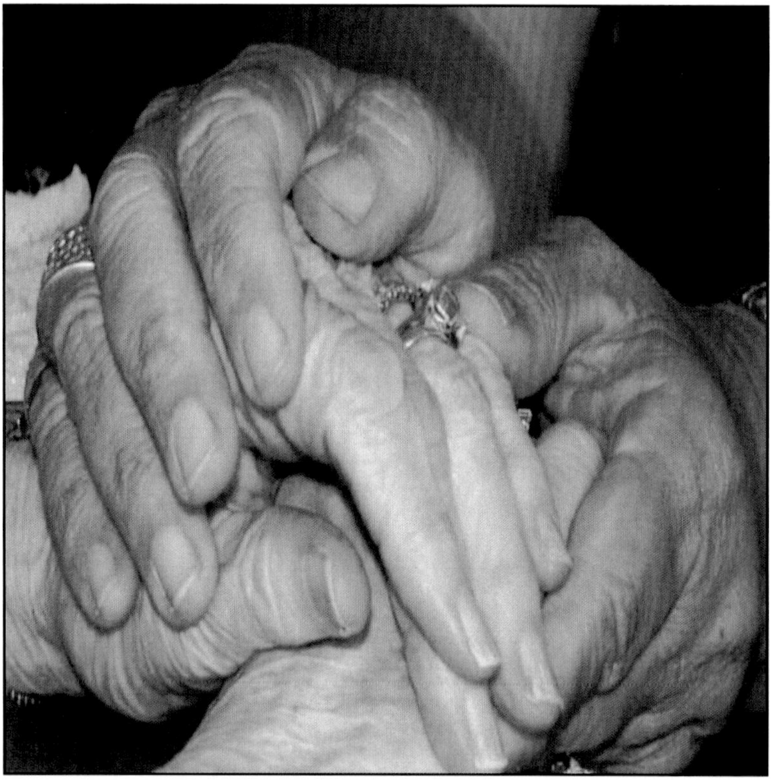

The most paralyzing emotion is fear,
which then elicits doubt and guilt.
It becomes immobilizing with dark emotion.
This darkness invades the body and takes
away its inner strength, power, and spirit.

Rise above the fear! Seize the moment!
The spirit and power are yours!

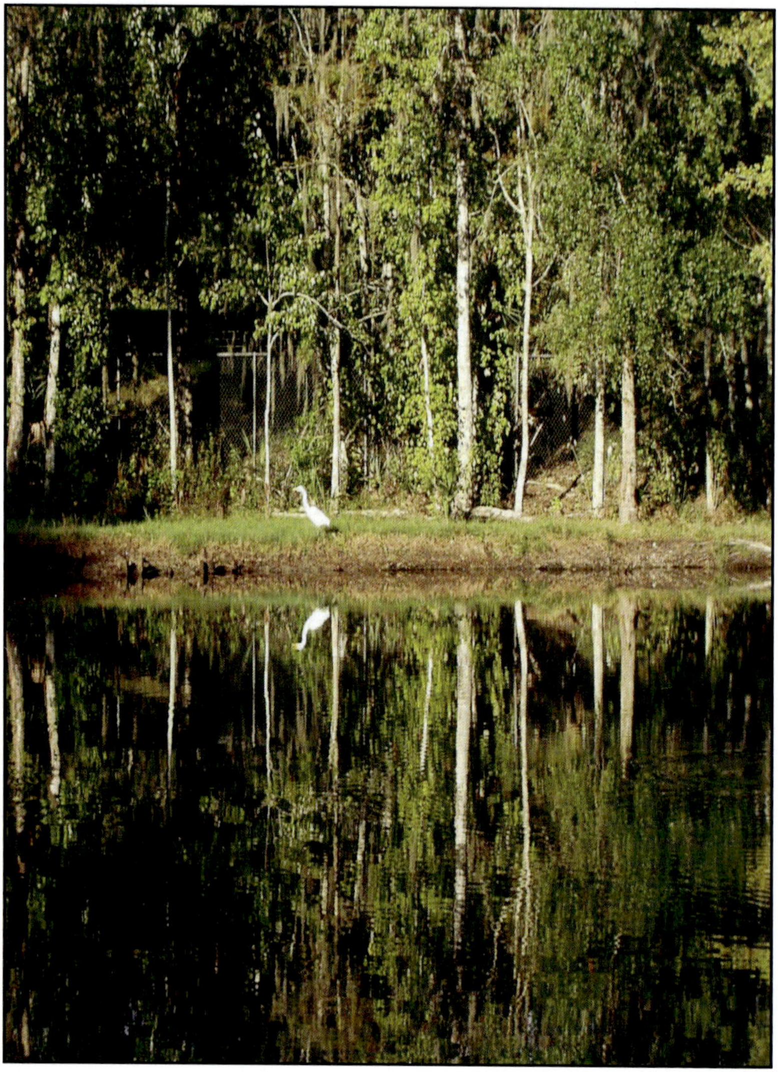

The ultimate gift is the simultaneously
and unconditionally mirrored
giving and receiving,
totally without thought,
with all your heart and soul,
from one being to another.

By giving the gift, in that moment
we become one, connected with a bond
so strong that it cannot be broken.

When a person receives the gift,
one can feel love, happiness, joy,
peace and tranquility.

This is the gift, it is the knowing.

Like droplets of water falling from the sky,
each one complete unto its self.
Each drop singing its song, vibrating,
touching all that surrounds
with its soft melodic music.

Then miraculously the drops form to
become one with another and another
until their song rhythmically crescendos
and flows into the streams and rivers.
They all are one, vibrating,
feeling the music.

The thunderous yet gentle composition
of this symphony will harmonize
to become the vast ocean. There somewhere
within this wondrous sound, I will always be.

Did you ever wonder why people greet
the morning differently than the night?
We wake up and say good morning
to the bright sun, the singing birds,
the colorful flowers and trees.
We are amazed by all the animals
and creatures scampering around.

But what happens to the night?
Do we greet the night while listening
to the voices? Do we look at the moon
and say good night in the same way
we say good morning, seeing the soft hues
reflecting from the moon light?
What about the depth and breadth
of the stars, reaching out into the
universe, asking us to join them?
The day-night is one.

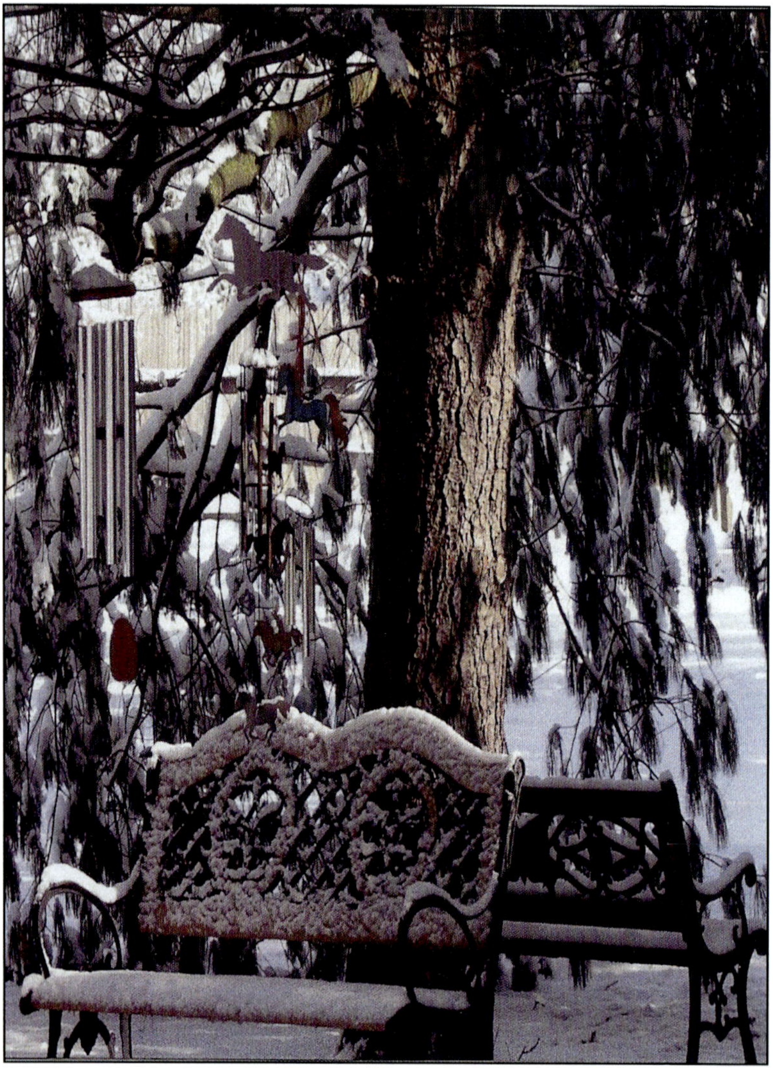

The road that I travel is a spiritual path
that connects my universal mind
with my higher self.

It is the path that searches for my pure being
and that of other kindred spirits.

I could not have found and
continued on this path alone.

You are the force and power of spiritual energy
that guides and encourages me along the way.

My experiences in life and awareness
of self and inner truth will always be
a part of this very special connection.

You are dedicated to sending peace, light and
renewed spiritual energy.

I will always greet your spirit.

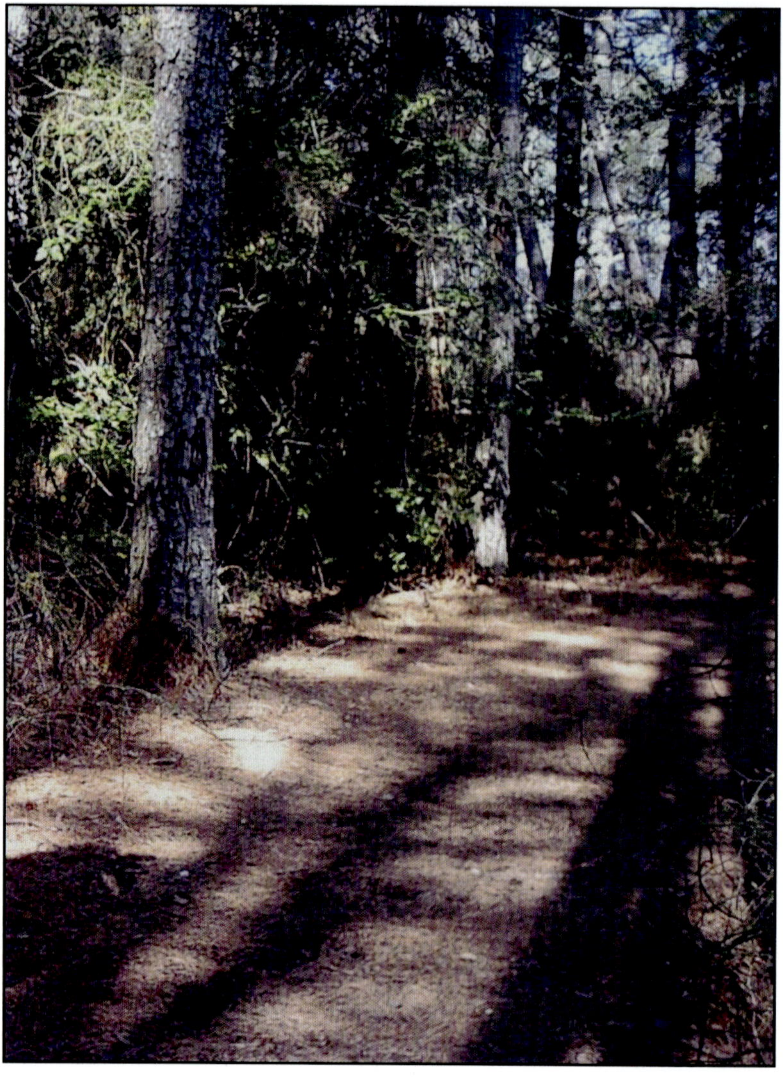

If you focus only
on the journey's end,
you will not be able to clearly see
the path that is in front of you.

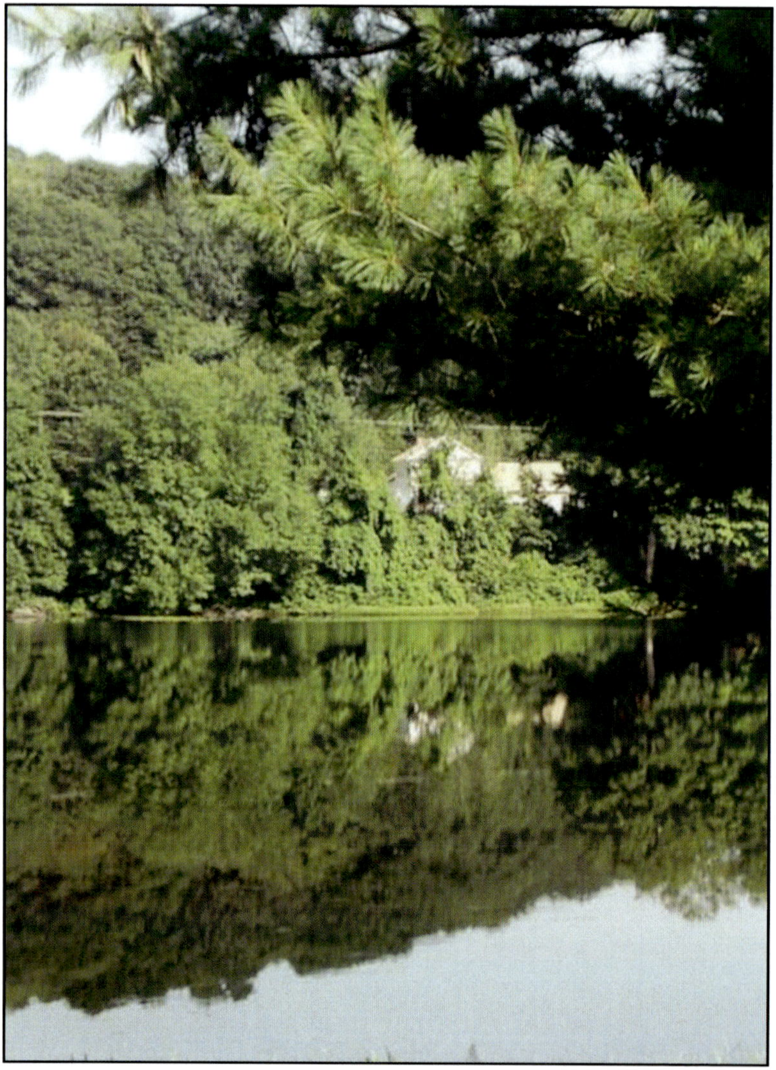

I am but a reflection of the universe.
But where I stand
in the light of day or night
changes that reflection.

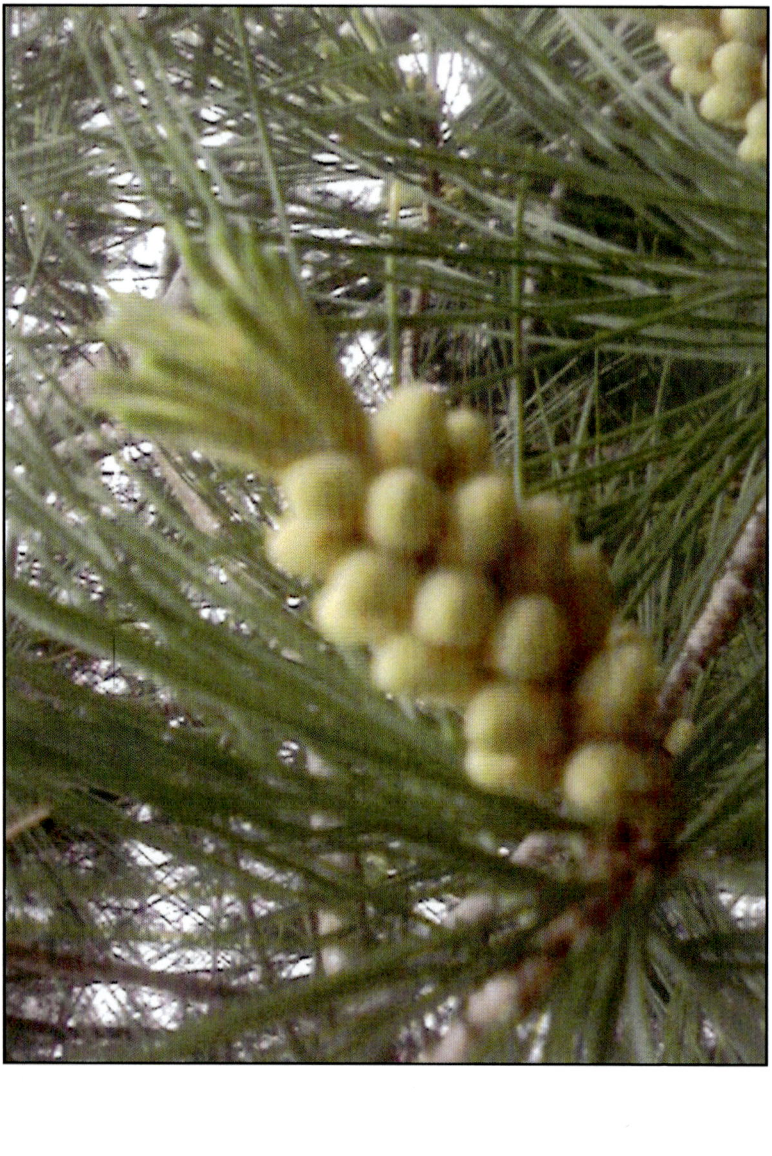

Although there are many wonderful
people in this world,
many do not wish to understand
what they have not personally experienced.

And do not wish to experience
more than they think they understand.

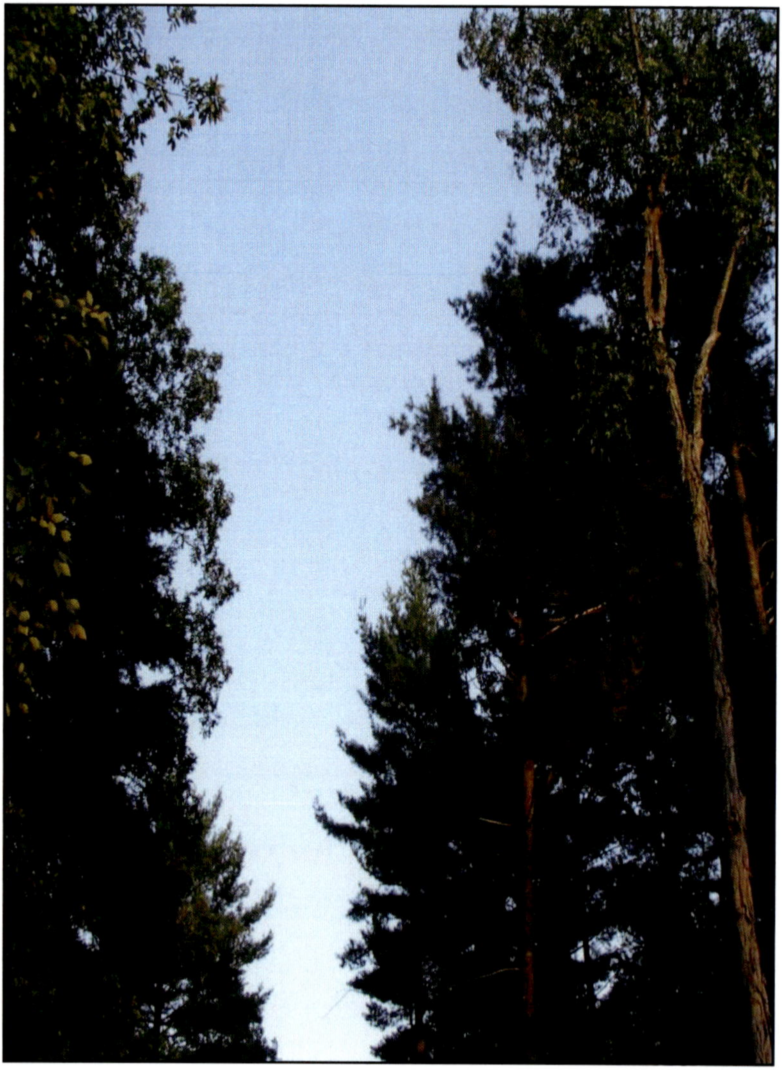

To find the answers of the universe, I must
know and realize the wonder of myself.

When I look within and then express my
thoughts outwardly, I have first gone
beyond the trees and the stars
and into the universe.

There is where I will find all treasures.
If perchance I do not find me out there,
then the universe is not.

But no worry.

I know and see what I have been
searching for is in the now.

That is how we evolve.
This is the moment.

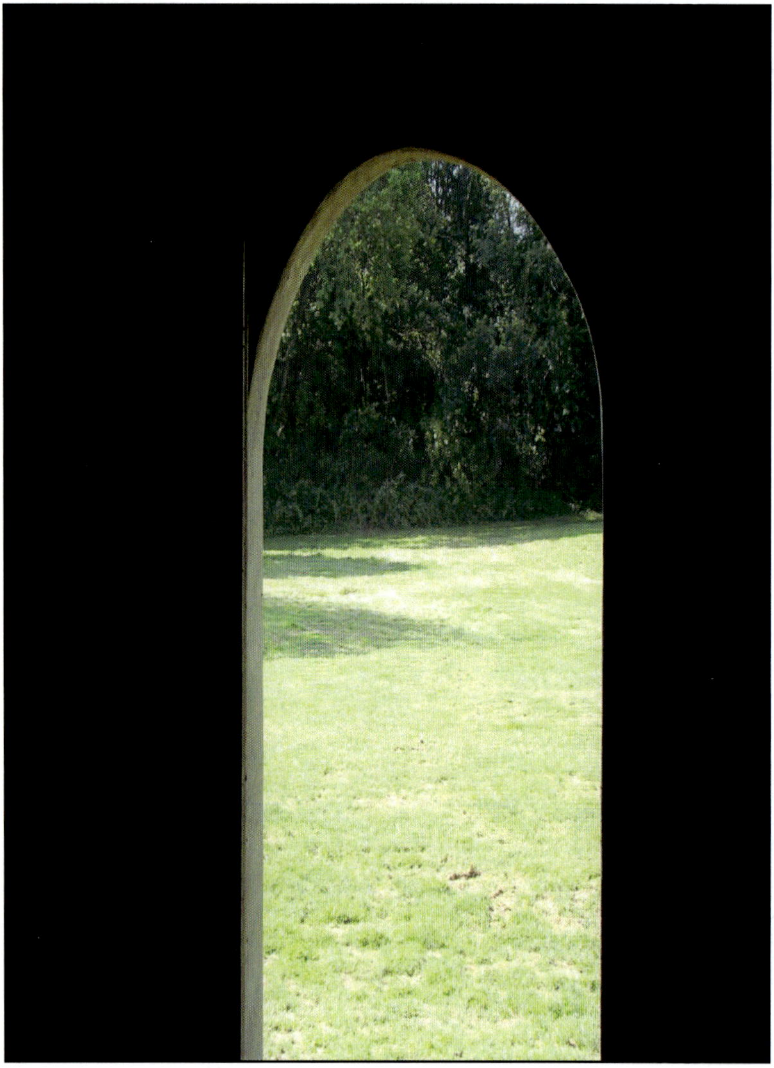

If you had a choice to be afraid
of either the unknown or the known,
which would you choose?

I would choose the known.

The unknown with its seemingly
out-of-control, eternal waiting, obsessing,
suffering, agonizing, and fearing over
what tomorrow may bring,
this is what drives man mad.

Tomorrow is yet unborn.
The unknown will not be known
until it is. This leaves the now moment,
that which is known.

The moment is here
and gone faster than fear.

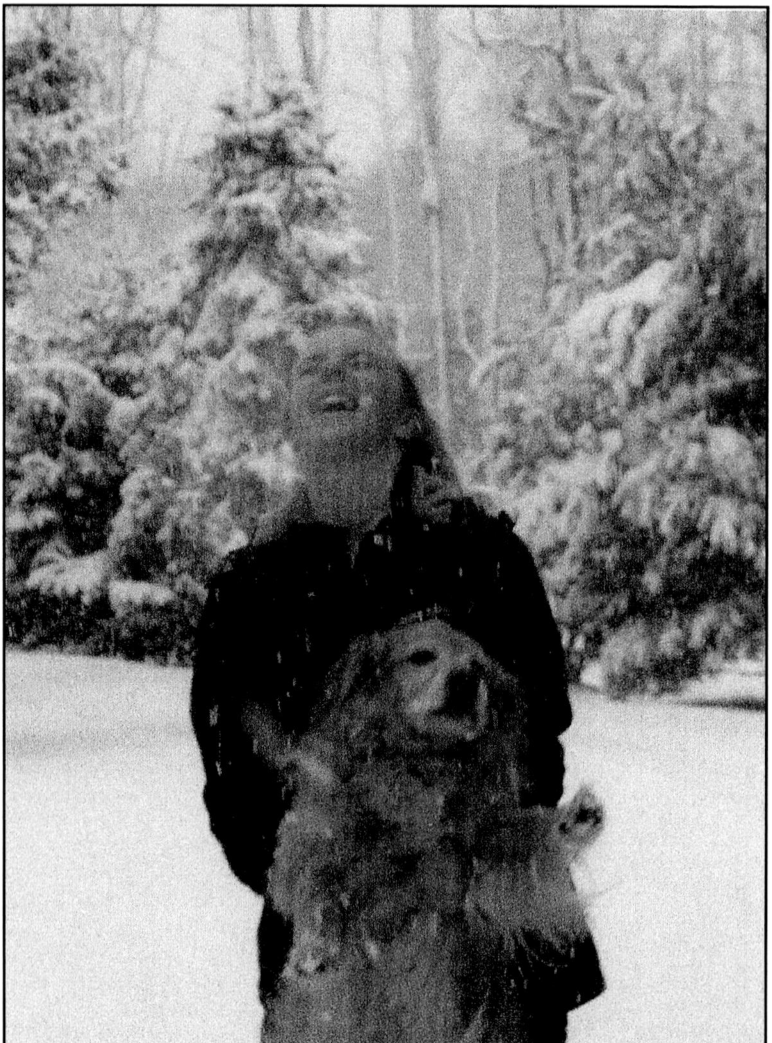

And when the winds blow so hard

from every direction,

so hard that I cannot stand any longer,

I close my eyes and see your vision,

know your strength

and believe.

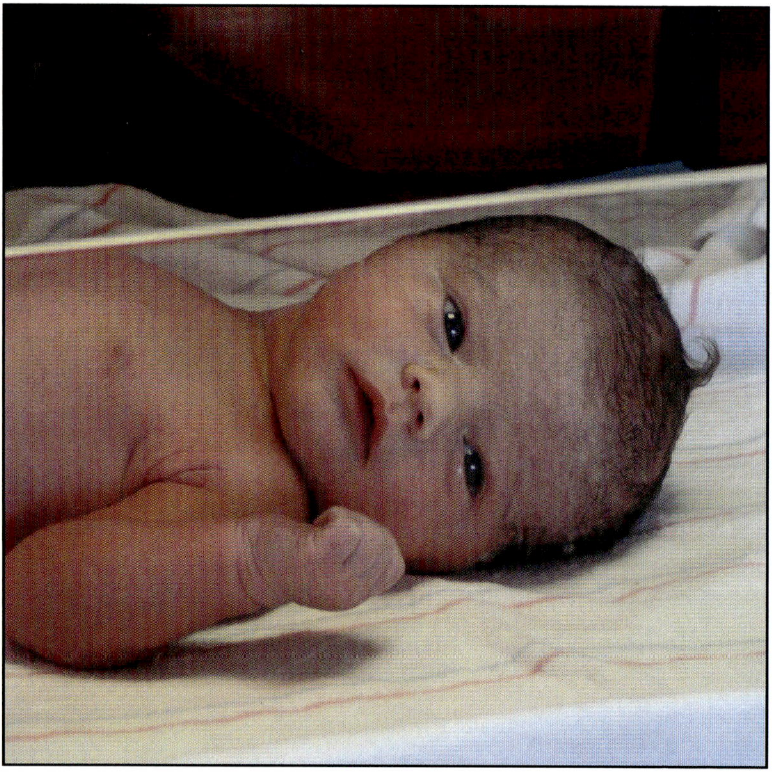

I have often been asked

if I ever wonder

whether other people understand

my words or thoughts.

Some will understand less,

but they are no lesser.

And some will understand more,

but they are not greater.

It just is.

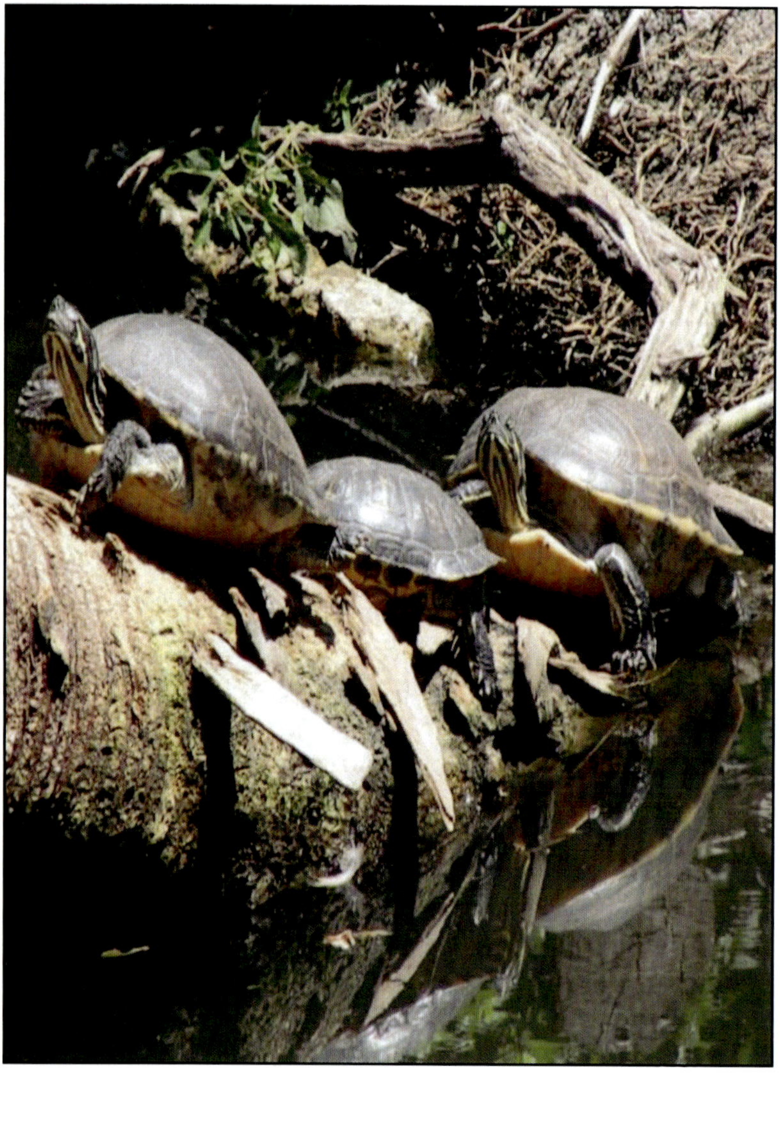

We all have natural abilities, intuition,
telepathy, space time travel.

They are naturally innate,
but suppressed throughout time.

We as energy forces are in a constant state of
change, reverberating at many different
frequencies at many different levels.

This is where we will experience the different
levels of enlightenment, going through
one spatial doorway, into another,
expanding and becoming, more.

I think from the time we are born,
we are taught that life is linear.

Go left right, right left, in out, up down.

Even the ladder of success is thought of
as up down, in a linear direction.

But just think when we were in the womb,
we were in total suspension, floating,
with all of our intended senses,
knowing infinity.

Even though we are in a finite space,
we are part of the infinite universal
vibration, and then we are born.

From that moment most of us spend our lives
just walking, thinking straight.

But there are some of us who will ultimately
find the space-time-beyond continuum.

There we will find a new dimension.

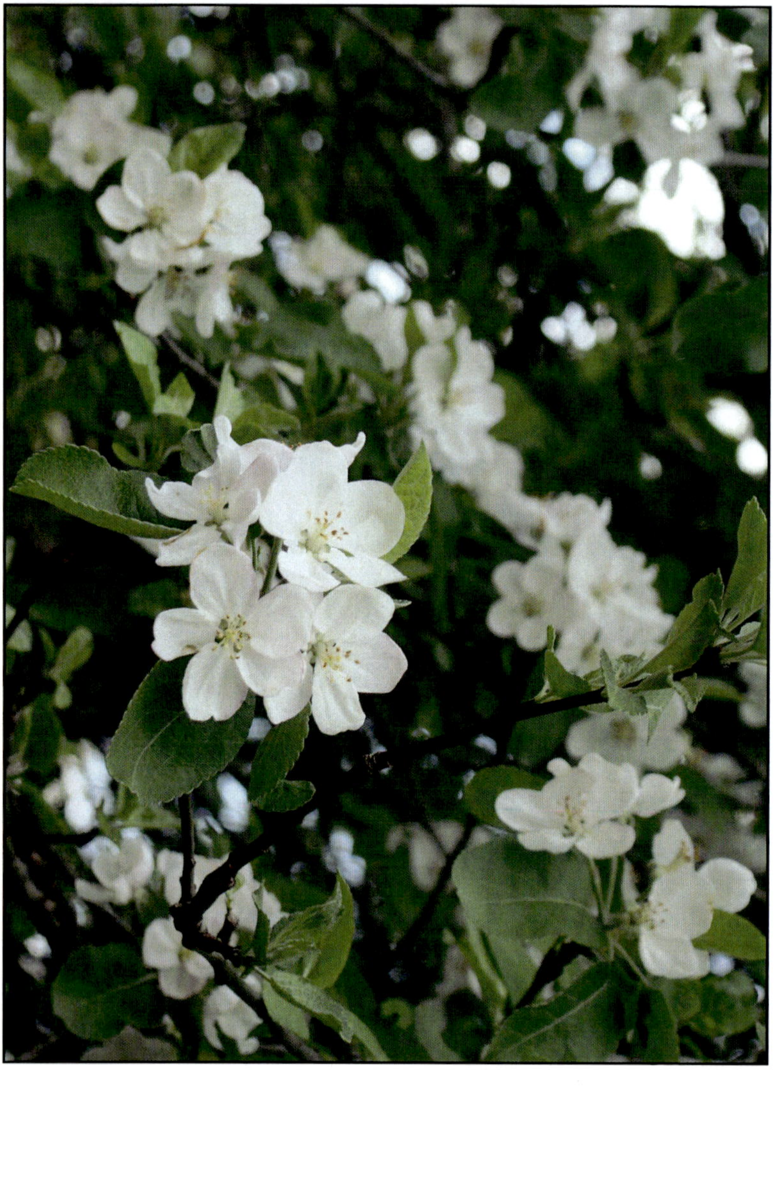

    Gently
        Lovingly
            Seeing
                Giving

Sharing
    Knowing
        Believing
            Being
                One

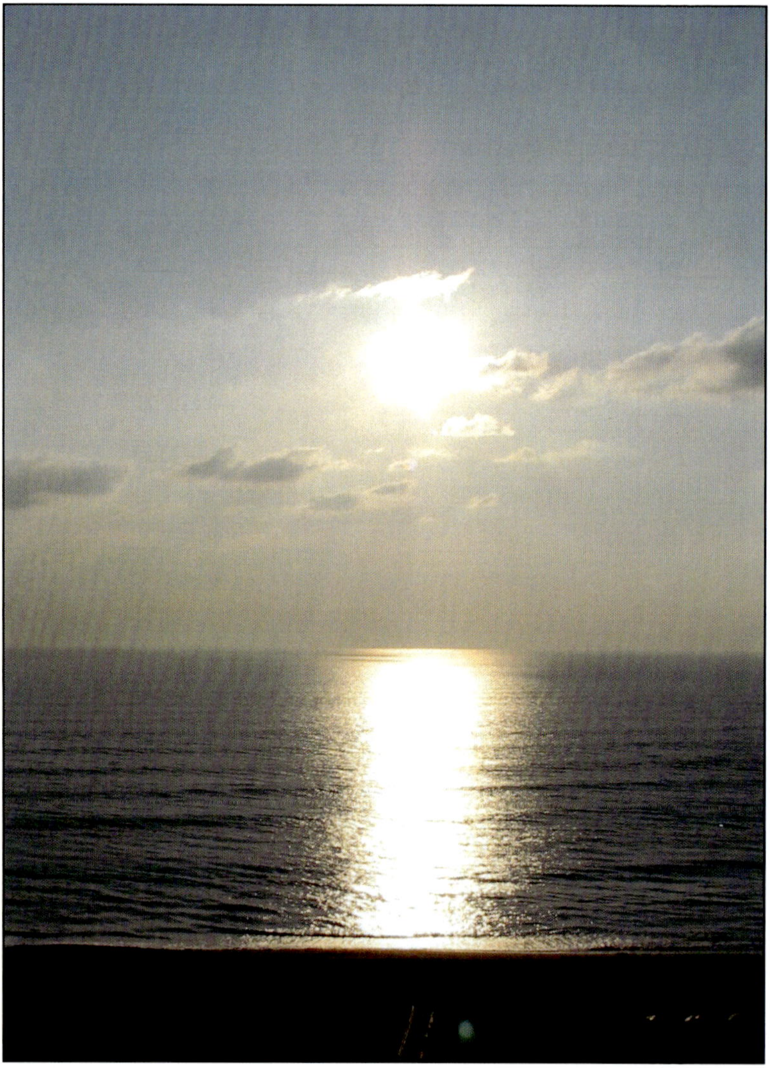

When one truly sees another's
inner soul, one sees all.

This soul illuminates all that is near,
creating a heavenly glow around them.

May we all have this
softness of light around us.

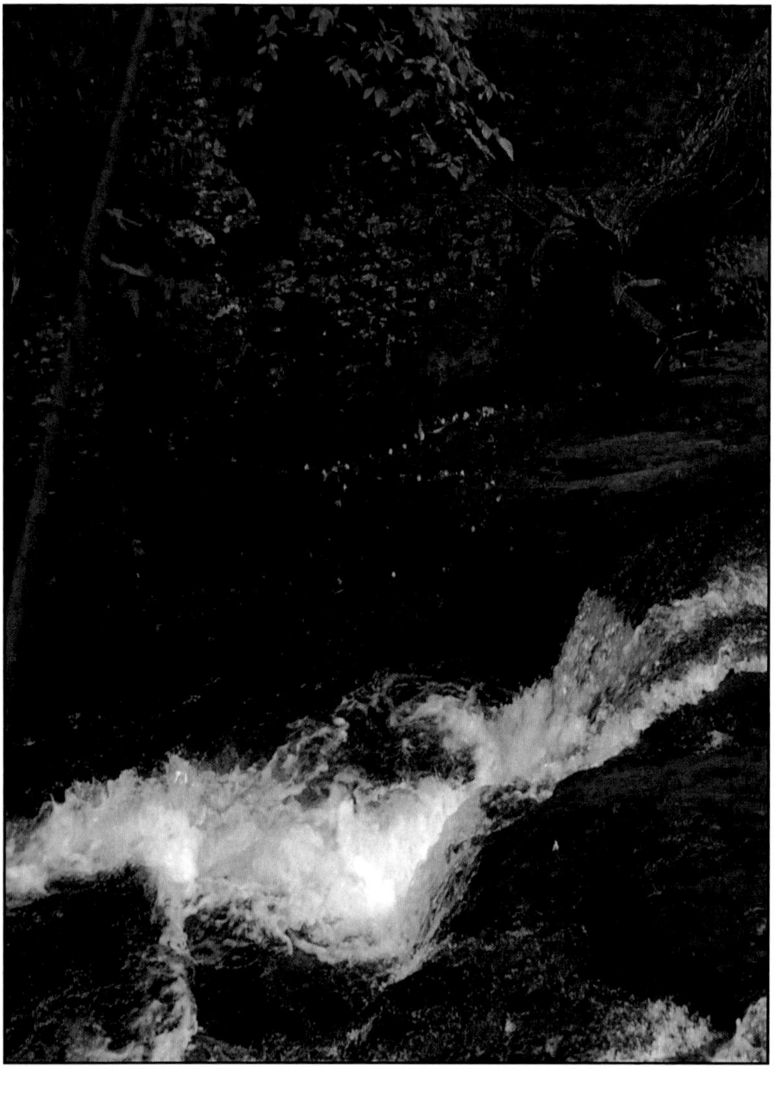

Sometimes my body, mind, and
spirit create a current of flooding
that crashes with such force, it is as if
they have become the uncontrolled
waters of a raging river,
breaking against its banks.

Trying to catch my breath,
I gasp and hold on until the waters
of the body, mind and spirit can be still.

One can flow with the raging waters
if they become part of its form,
accepting, interconnecting, knowing.
Although One, there is an individual
beauty that is separate and unique.

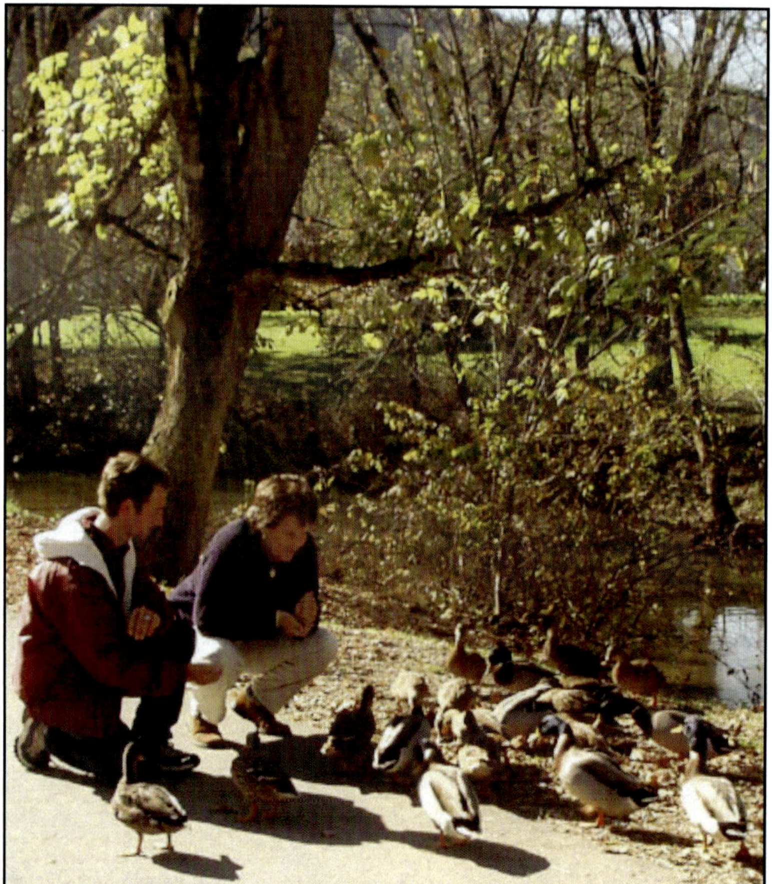

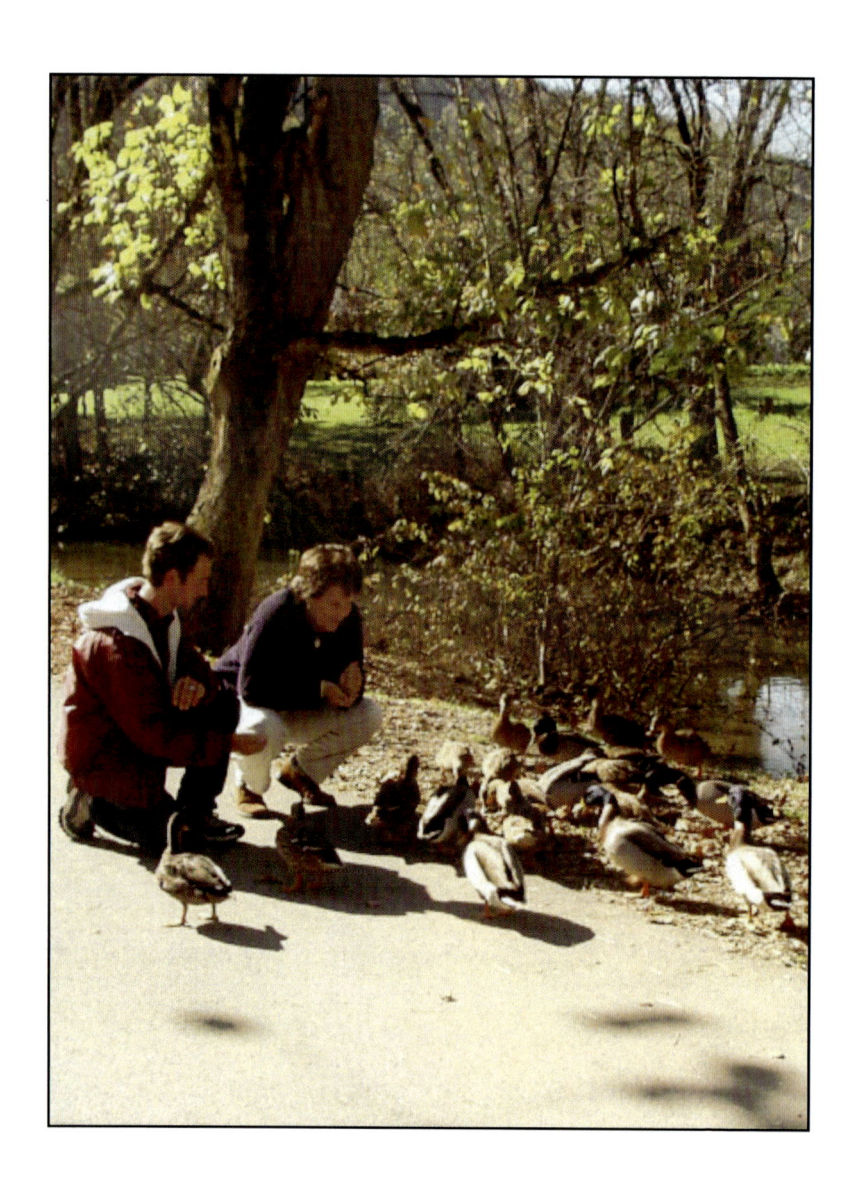

By understanding our

complete relationship with

ourselves and other living things

we can obtain harmony

in our daily lives.

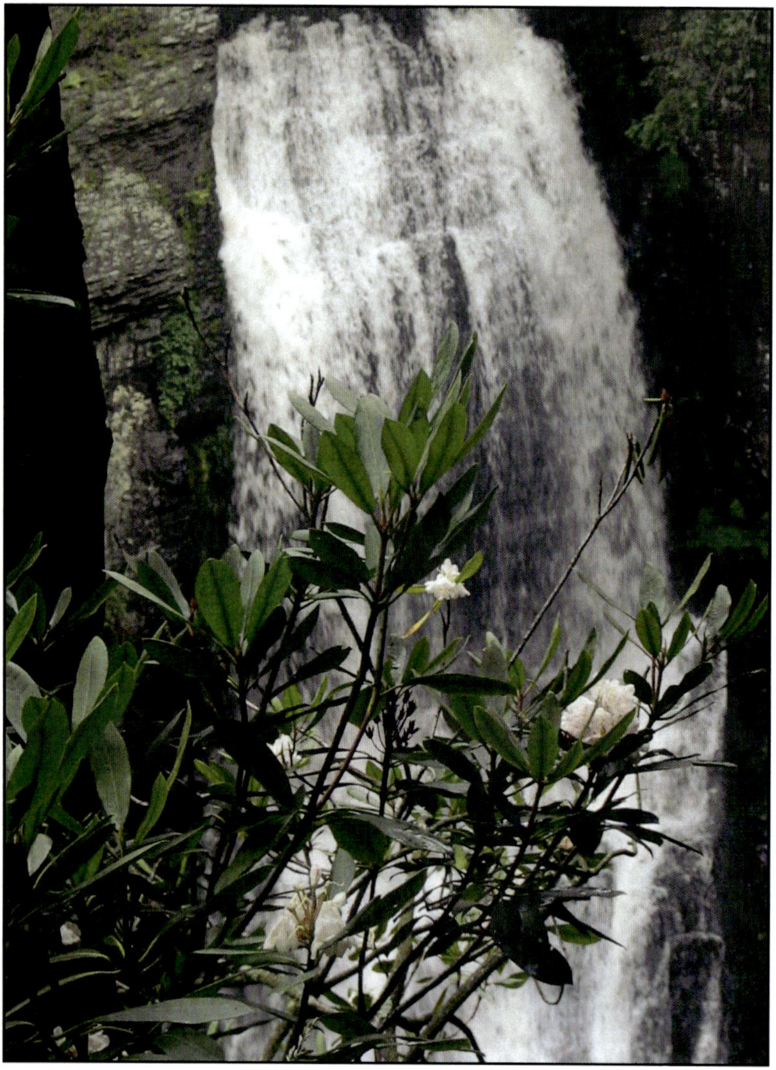

What is life
but to create music
in our hearts and souls
so that the universe
can hear our symphony?

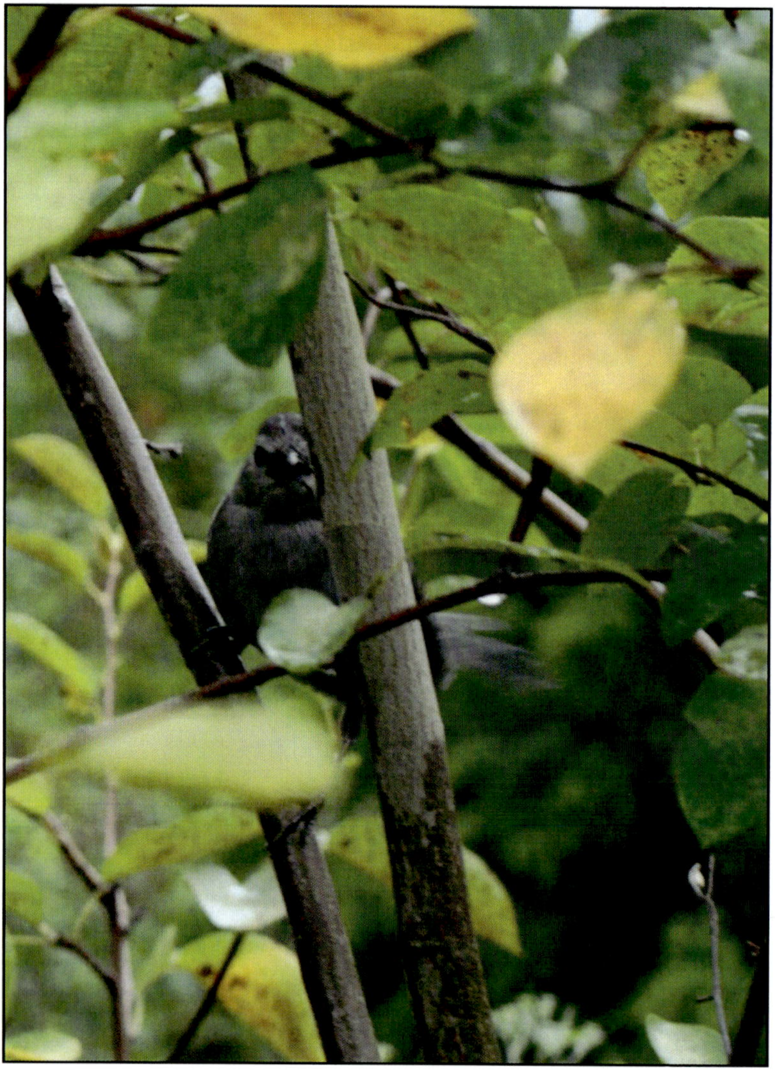

Greater than words from others
 are the words
  I hear and sing
   within myself.

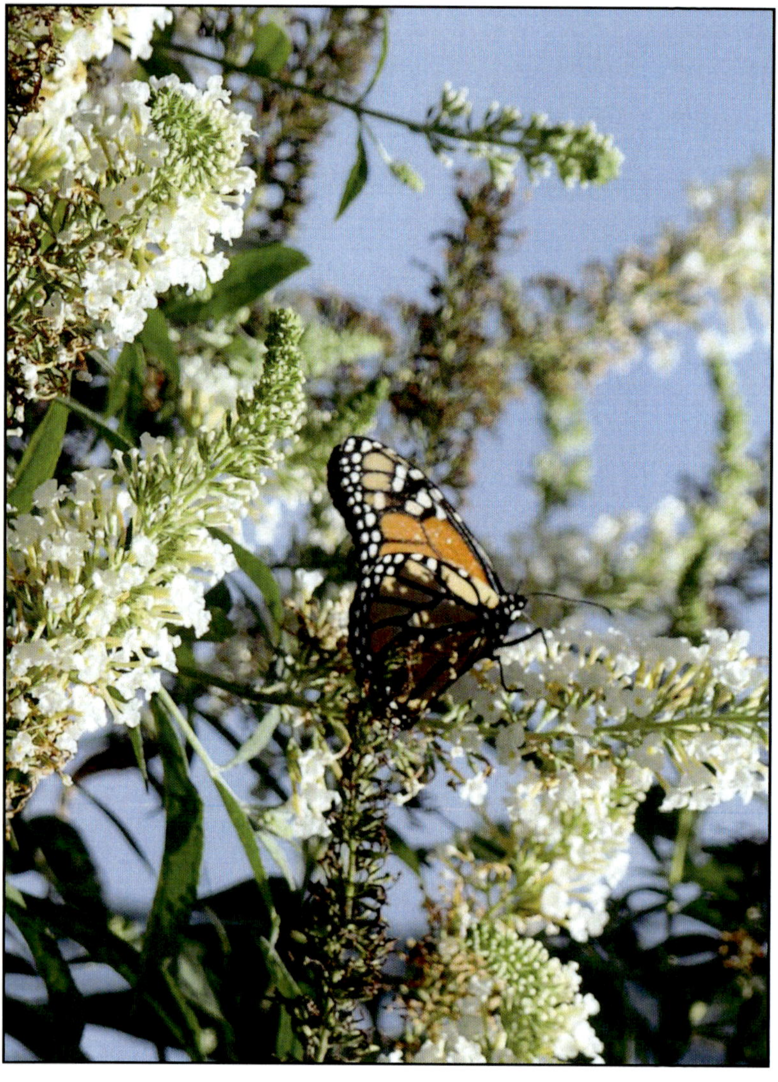

If a focus in life

becomes the only goal,

then the gratitude

for all of life

will be lost.

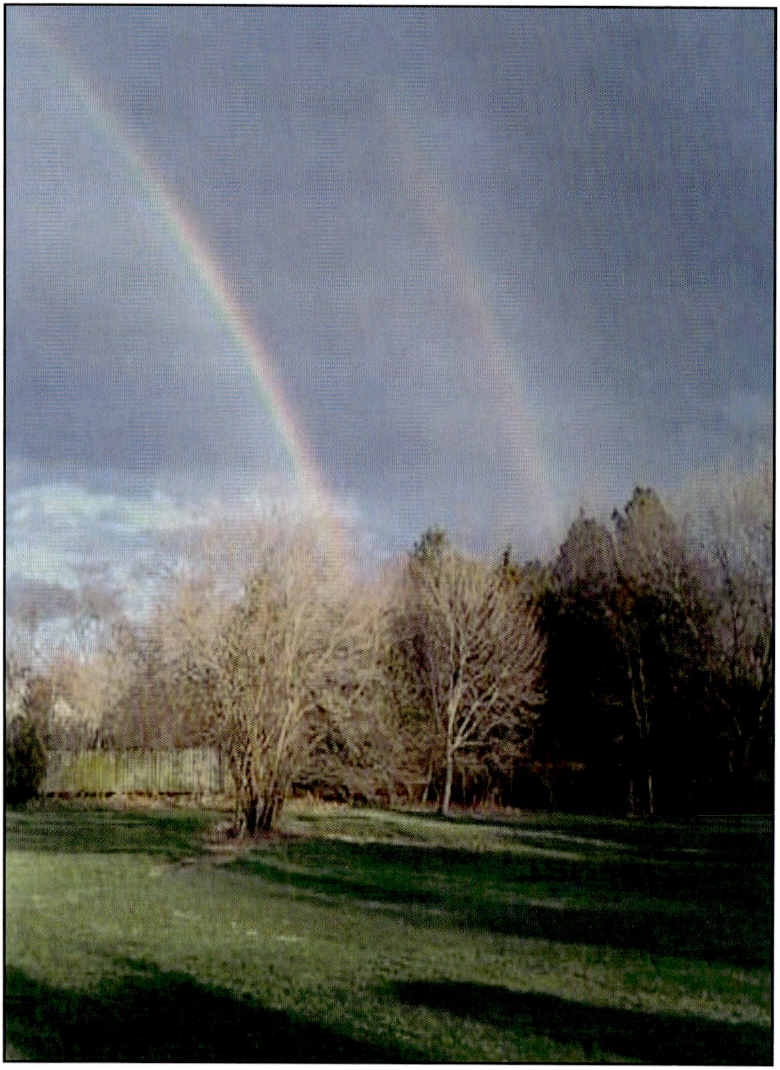

Behold the universe,
the beauty that resides in all of us!

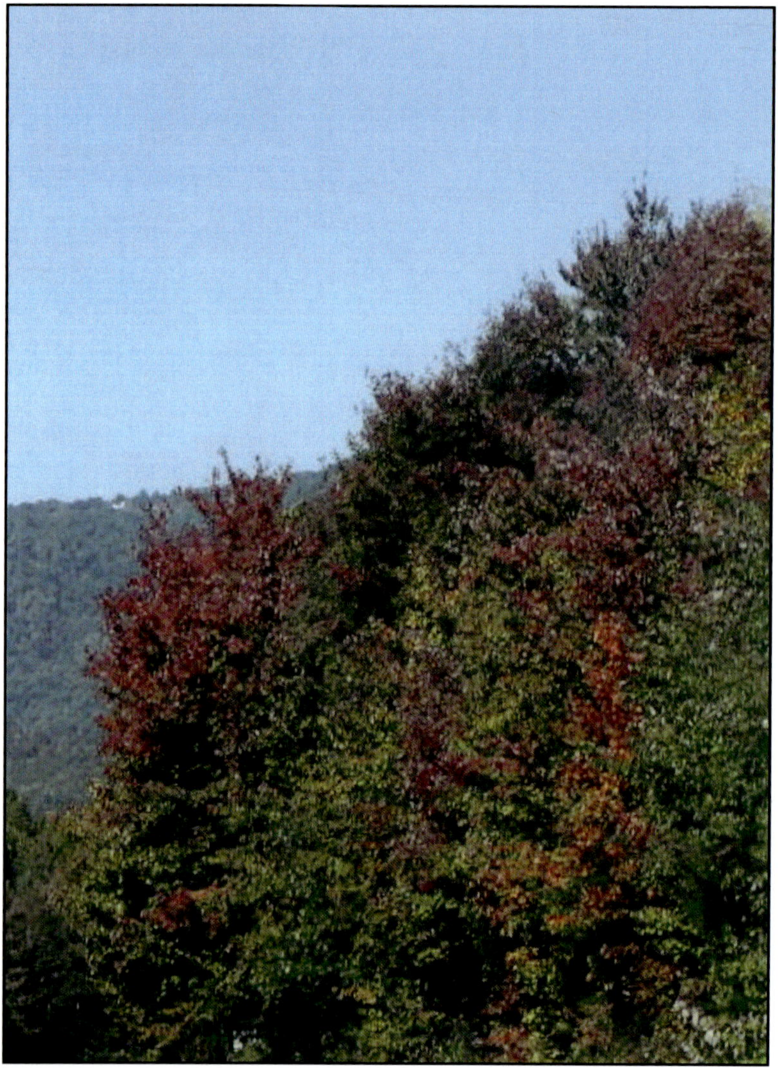

Life is a beautiful colored cloth,
and every living breathing thing
is a thread interwoven into this cloth
to create a wonderful tapestry.

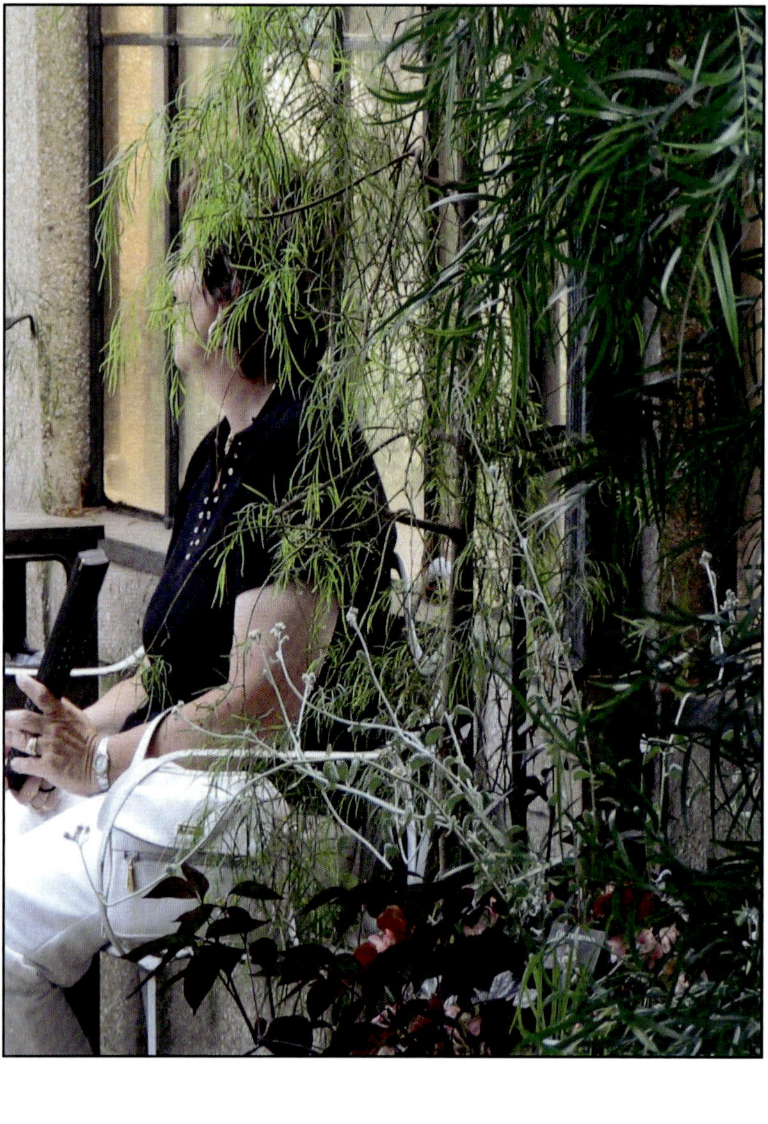

The glory of prayer is
when one prays the vibration created
echoes softly throughout the universe.

If in this moment of stillness
the words that are uttered
come from a pure heart
with pure intent,
one will be able to feel
the quiet peace.

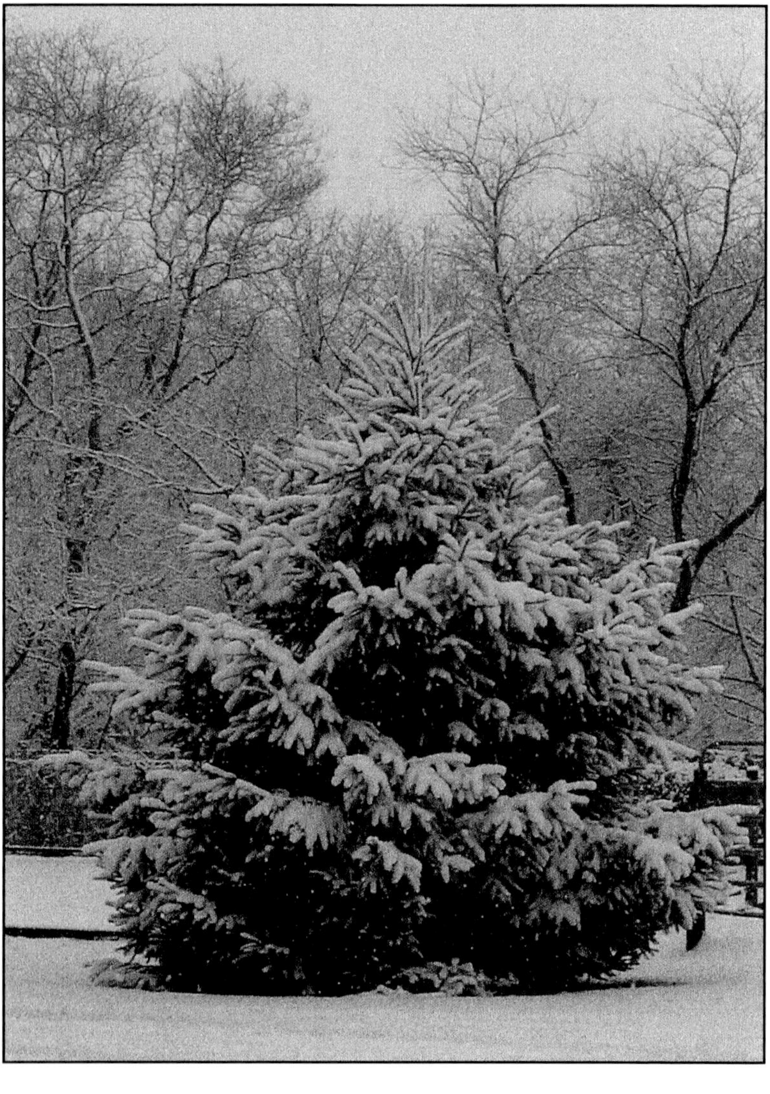

Once you have seen,
you will always know.

Once you know,
the connection will always be.

Sometimes while walking through life,
the sky gets dark, clouds form, and
an unavoidable storm will be upon you.

Any storm becomes a challenge
for how one will conquer the seemingly
unbearable burdens of
yesterday, today, and tomorrow.

There is no life without storms,
no storm without the emotions that
can shake the very belief of our inner soul,
if we allow it.

Believe,
This is the moment,
and in this moment is the new lighted path.

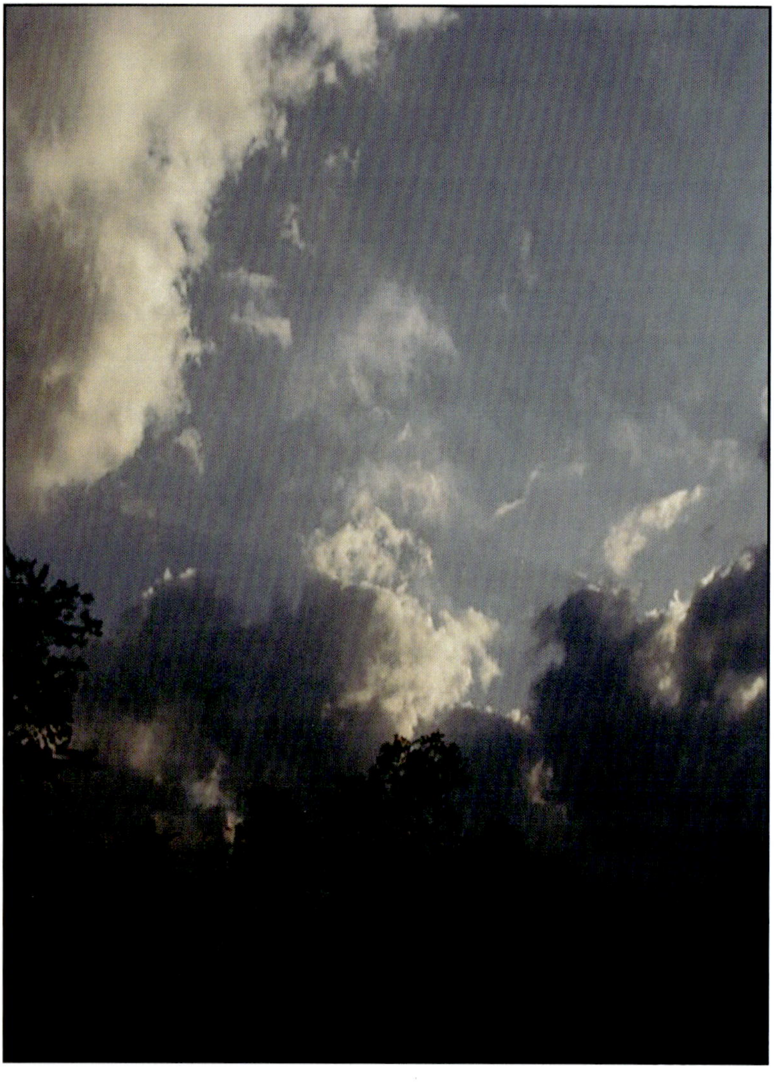

It started from a distance,
the winds calling to each other,
beckoning to become one.

Sometimes, when I look up into the skies,
I yearn to know what it is that I truly see.

Is this a vision or just the magnificence
within the skies?

Then for a moment, a fleeting moment,
I realize the seeing and knowing is in
the beauty of that moment.

This is what carries one away.

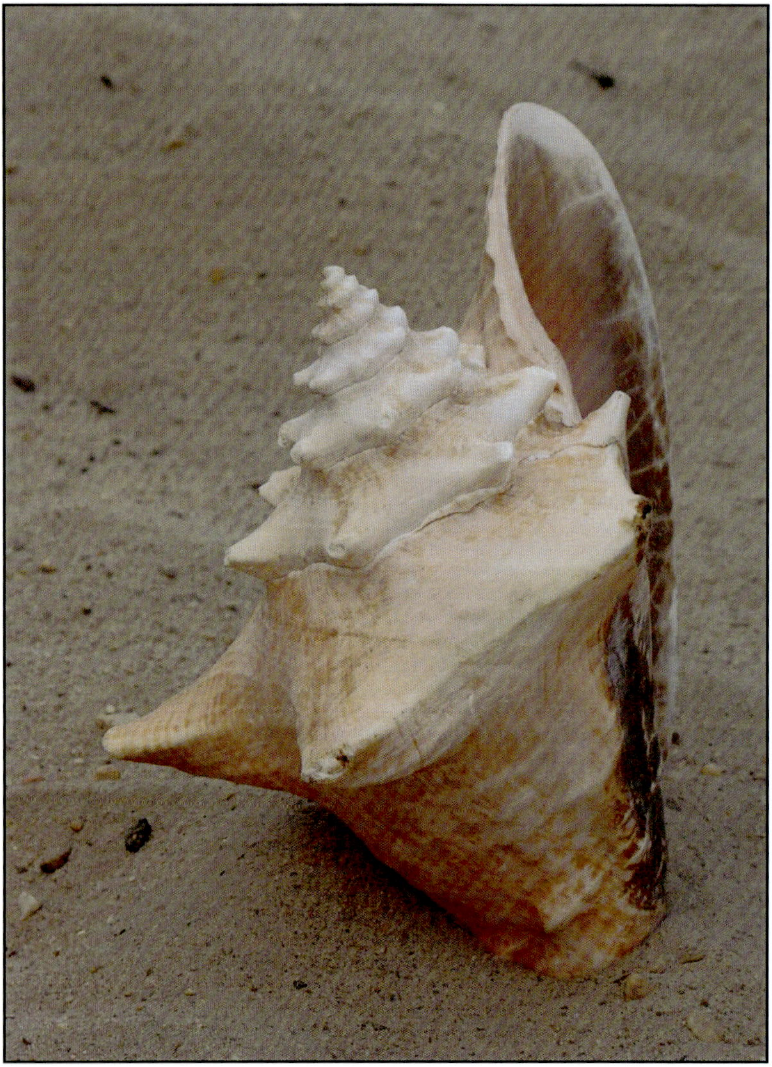

To truly see, takes more than sight.

To hear, takes the reverberation and translation of the universe into a language that is all its own.

To touch, one must reach out and touch gently with all your heart and soul.

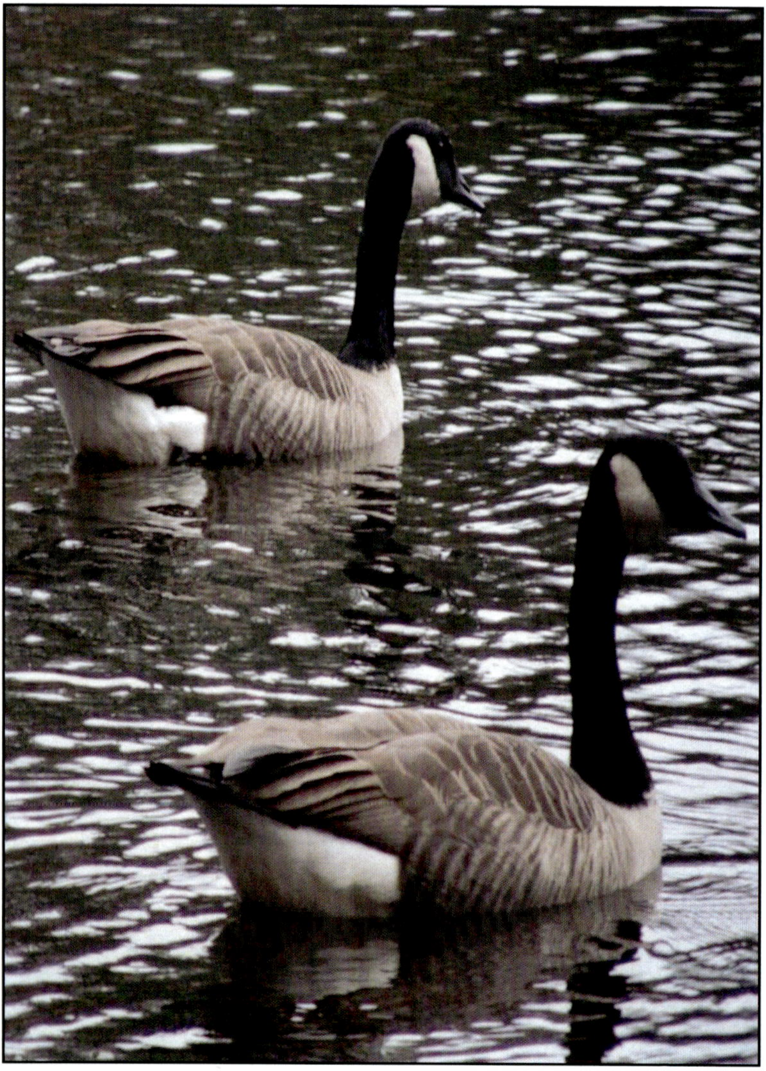

I whisper in your ear and you hear my
dreams and aspirations.

You sing to my heart whenever we are near.

I sing back in refrain, our voices becoming one.

My spirit will always dance with your spirit.
Our spirits will always dance together.

Once connected, we can never be apart.

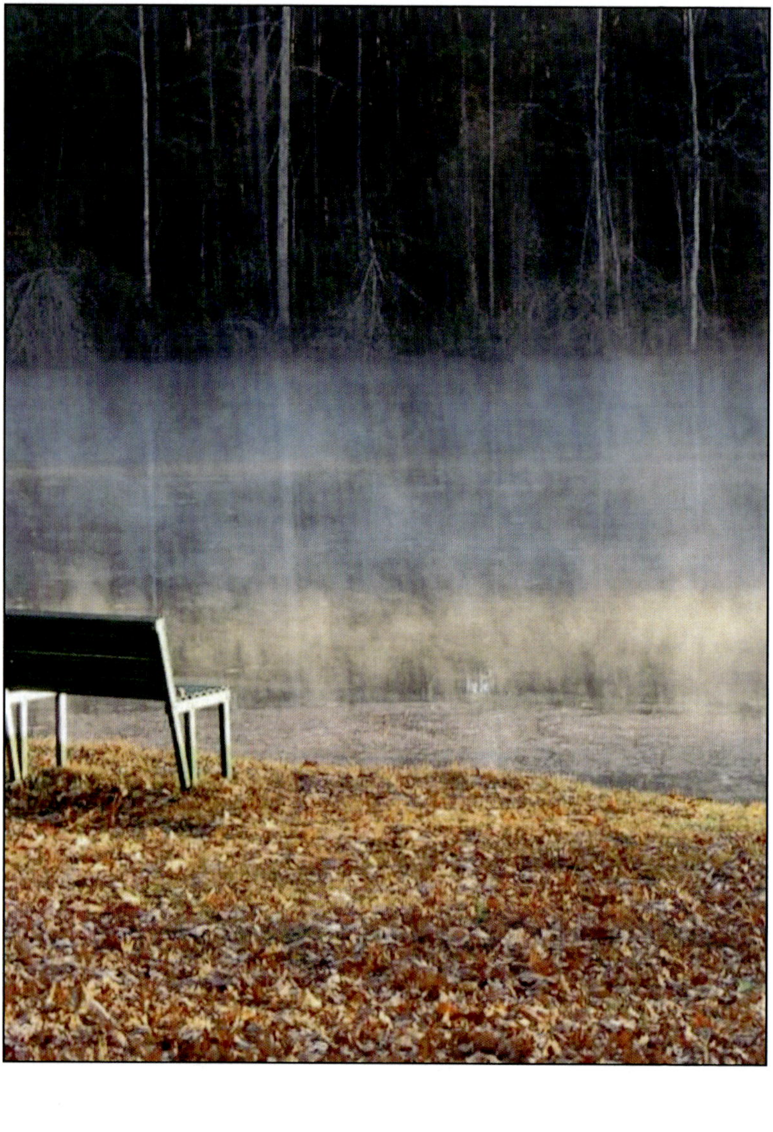

Today and every day I wish for you
to always be embraced
with peace and stillness.

I wish for you the continued vision
to see all of life,
in all its glory,
with the splendor of surrounding colors.

I send to you the warmth and beauty
that radiates from those colors.

And may you always be blessed
with spiritual energy.

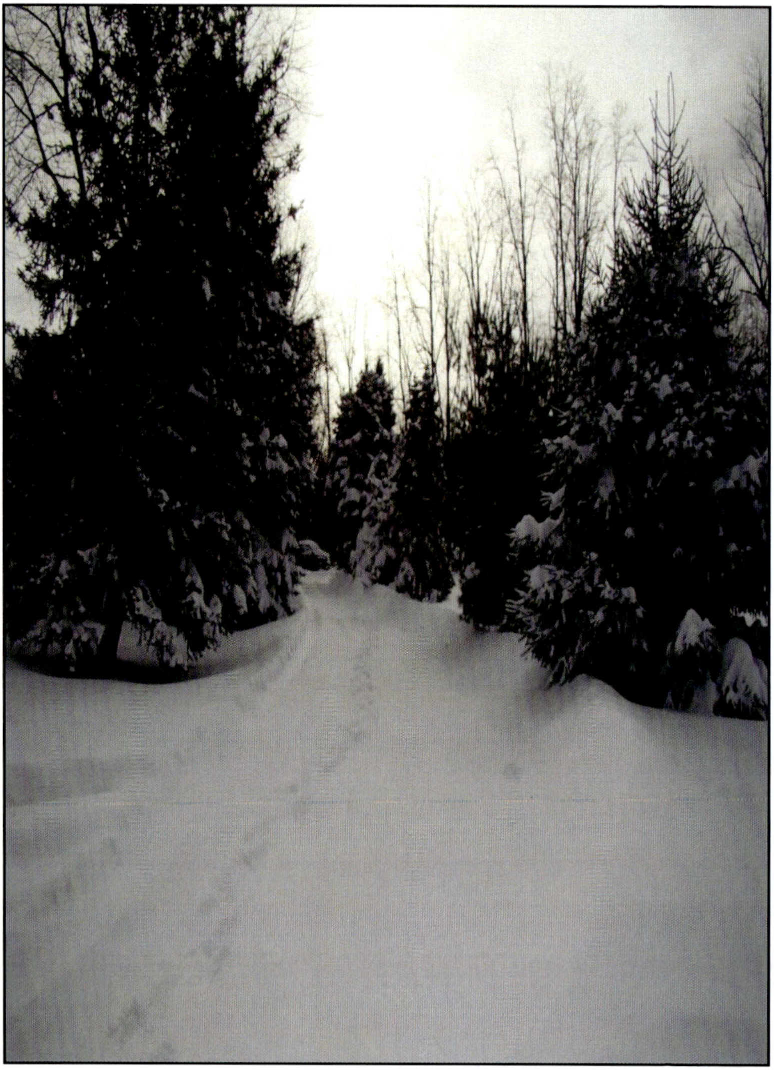

In life we will travel the path
that some may call our destiny.
Along that path, at times,
we may walk alone or with others.

Sometimes we walk alone because
it may be difficult for the ones we care for,
or those who care for us,
to see or understand
the vision of the path we must take.

Know, as I am sure that you do,
that you will never walk alone.

Your faith, strength, and spirit
are always with you.

And this human spirit,
that believes in all that you are and will be,
will walk the path with you,
in trust and friendship.

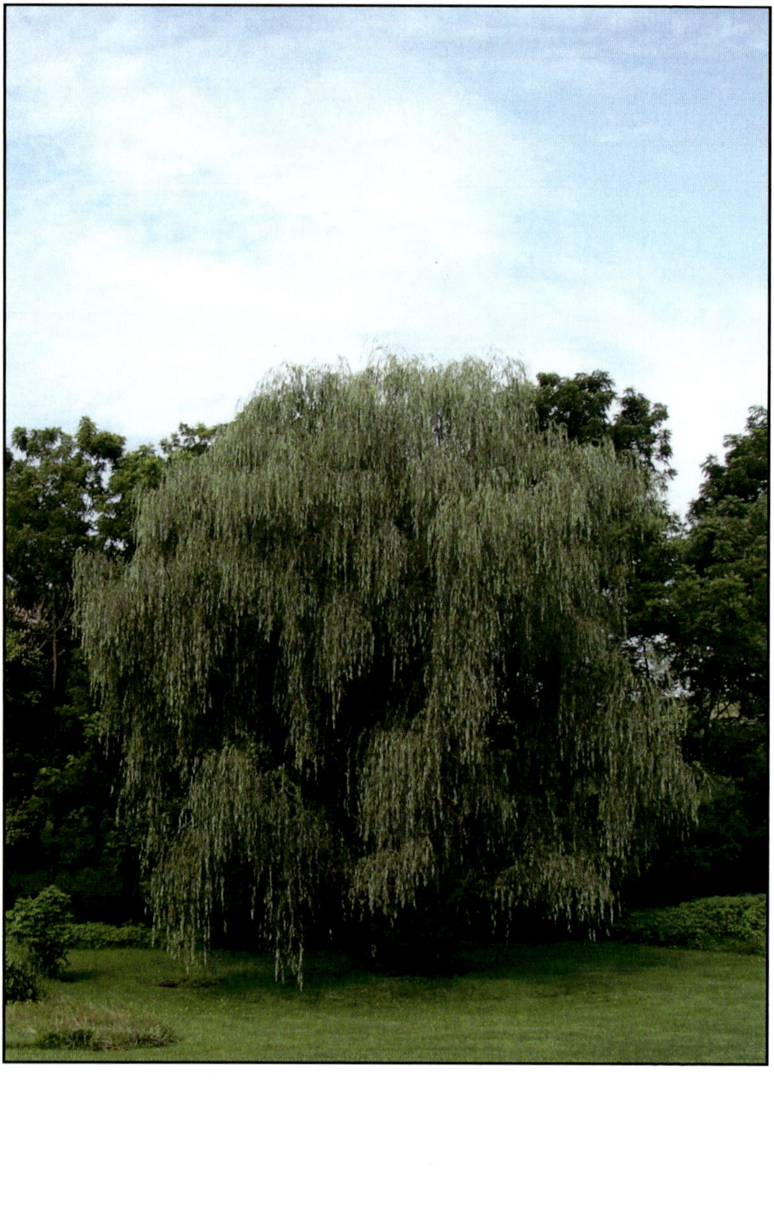

I know that I am different from many,
but I am also the same to a few.

That sameness creates a surge,
an energy in my life
like no other life experience,
so that I may become.

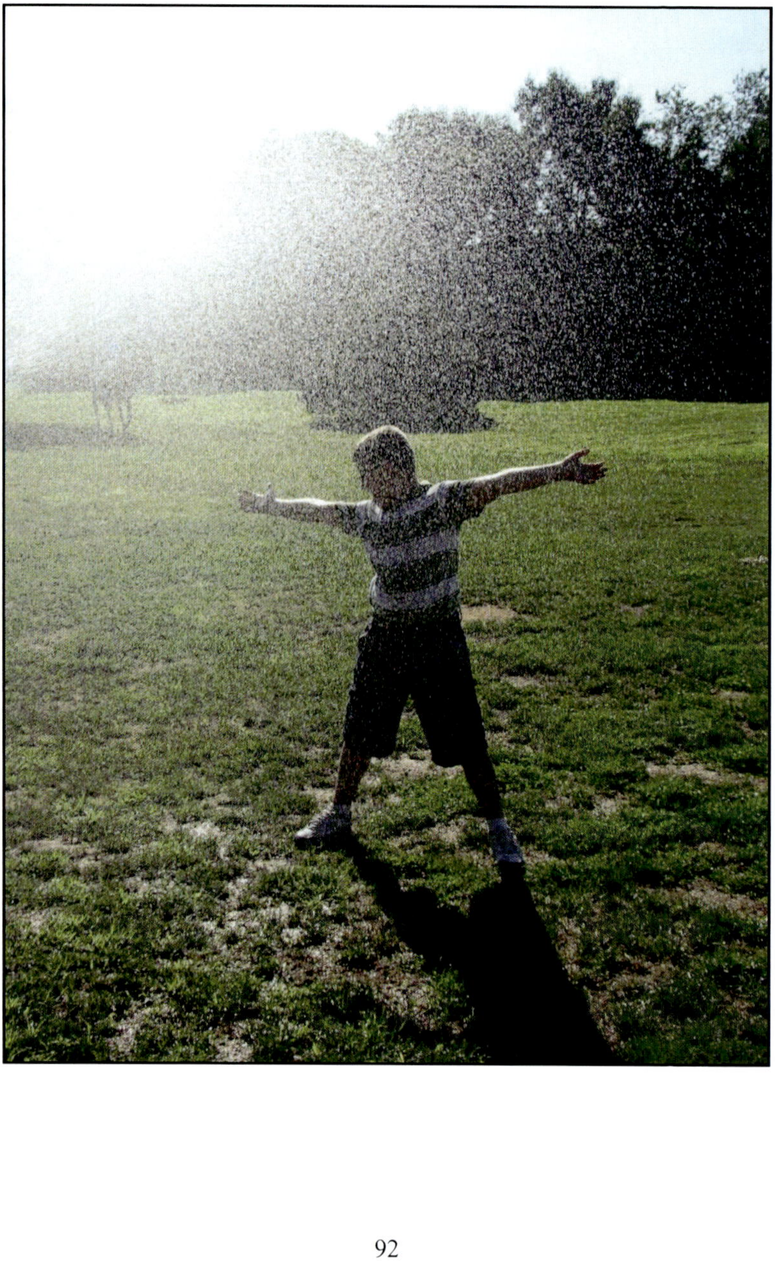

Dance with the rain drops.

Know the warmth of the sun
from within all souls.

Fly with the wind and spirits
to depths unknown.

See the reflection of the rainbow
within myself and all.

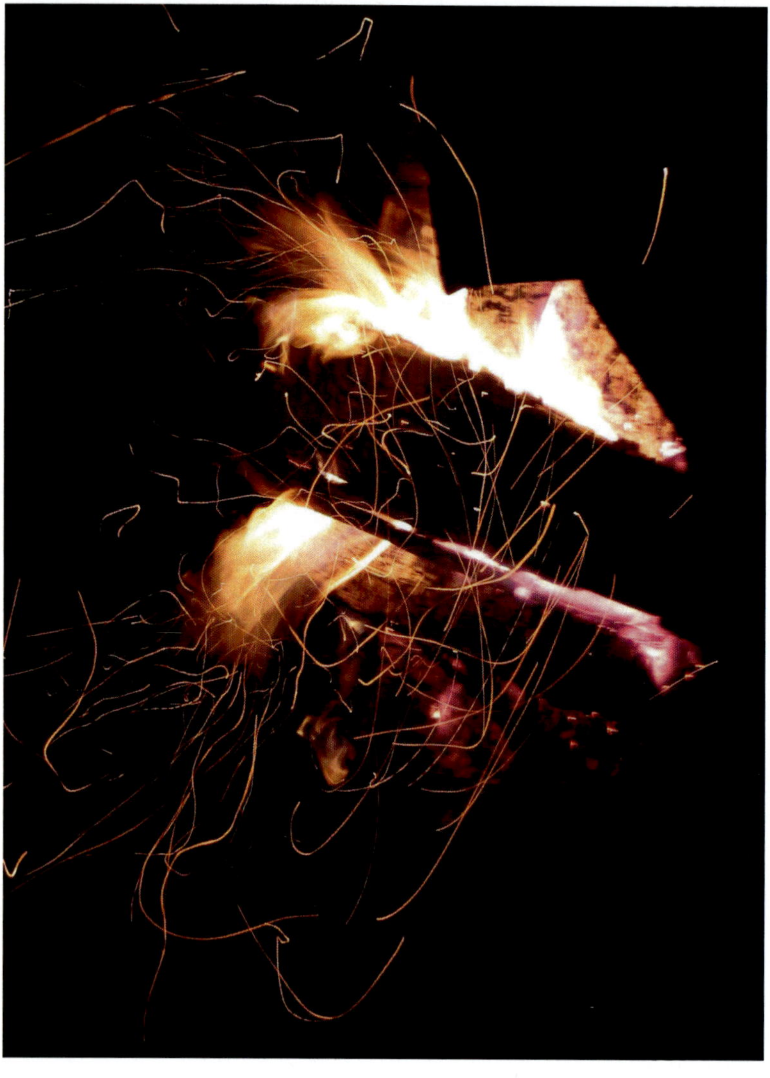

The illusion

With its grasping and shadowy touch,
the night that speaks so much.

Light that becomes the dark, and
withdrawal that beckons the heart.

With fear that stokes the fright
of the abyss within the night,
it is but an illusion.

Go softly into this night,
the fear will be alright,
as the dark becomes the light,
and we find ourselves this night,
and know it is just an illusion.

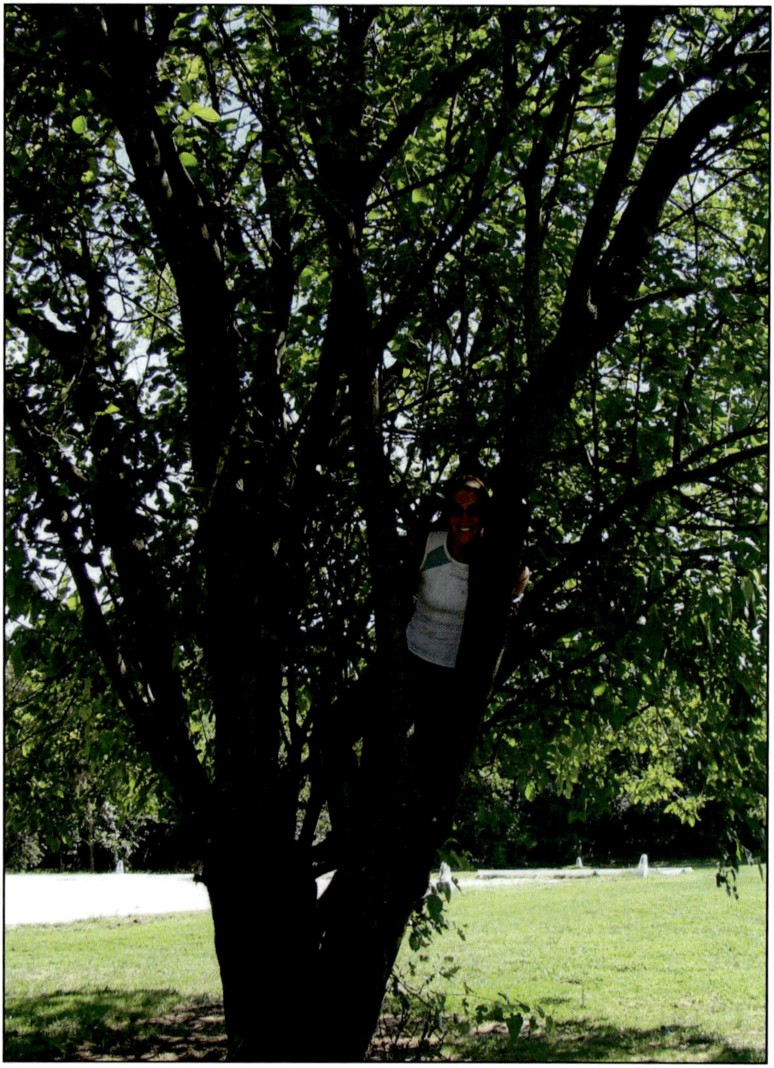

I am but a reflection of you
as you are of me,
and all are of the universe.

The body, mind and spirit although one,
grow independently of each other
like the outreaching branches
of a blossoming tree.

Although the branches are separate
they are connected,
as they find their nurturing roots
from the earth and present their
gift of life to the heavens.

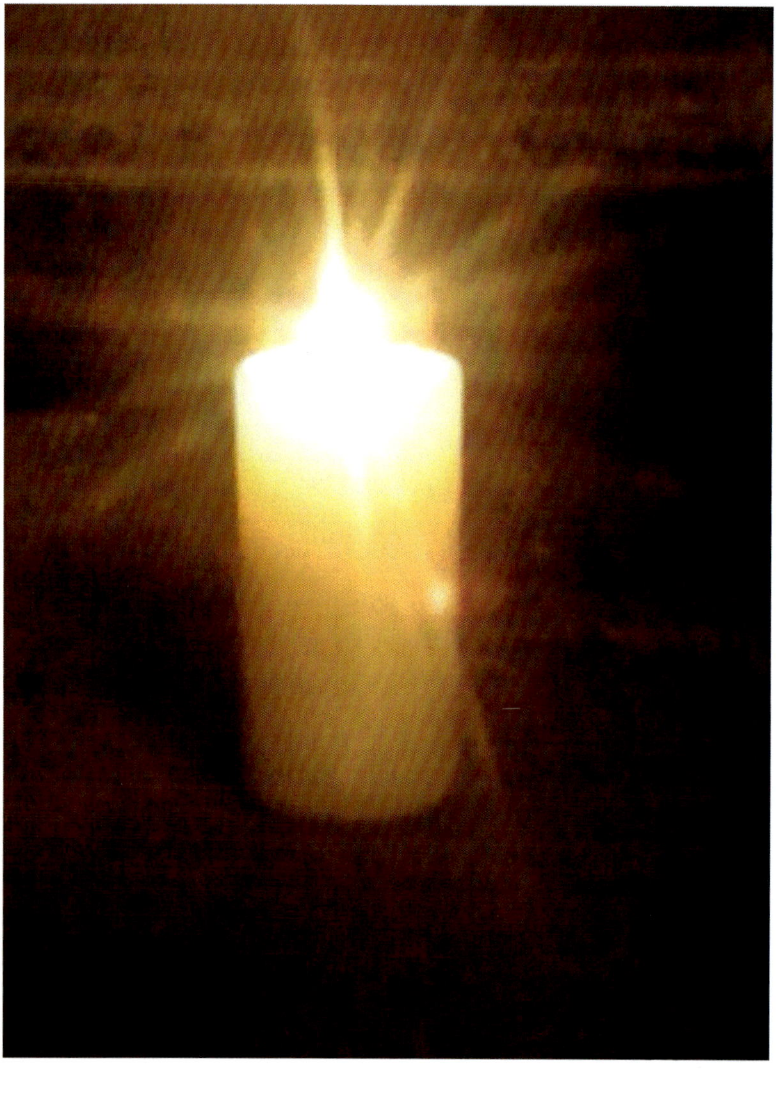

The Light That Glows Within

One light
glowing from within one spirit
can illuminate tens, hundreds,
even thousands of other spirits,
and never will it be diminished
by doing so.

This special, unconditional light
radiates kindness and love.

The inner light shines brightly,
not only for a few,
not just for the receivers,
but also for the giver.

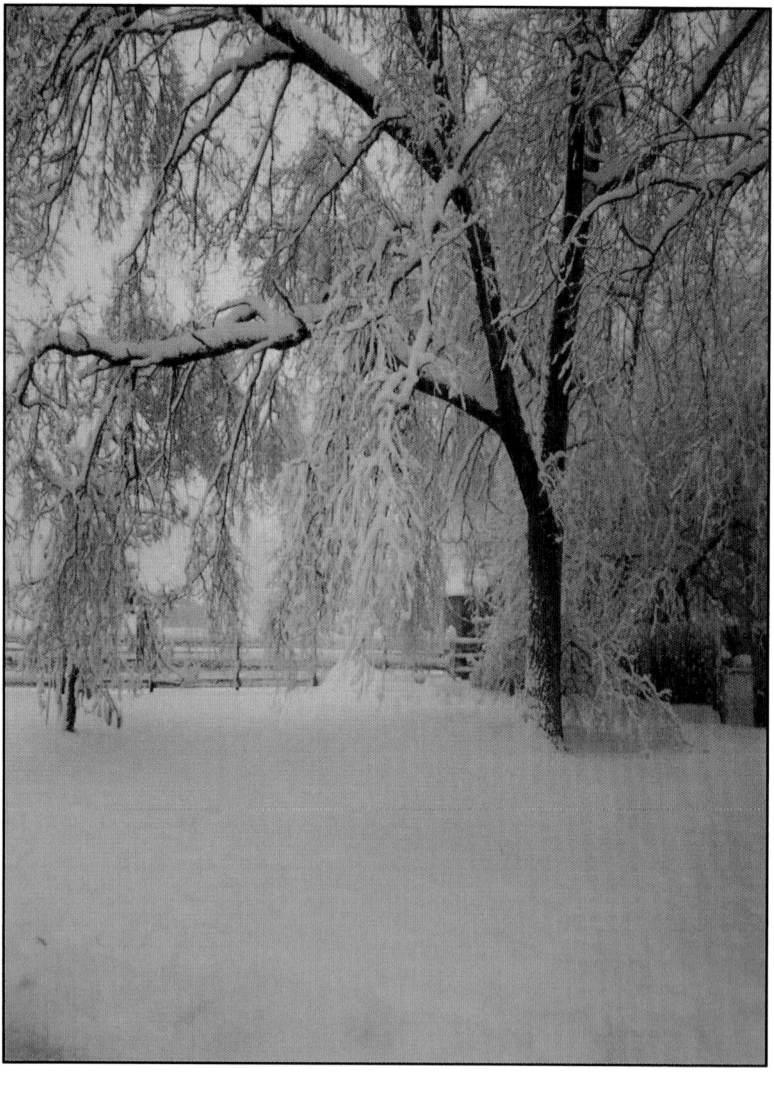

Gratitude helps one to affirm
and acknowledge the inner self,
the outer self, and beyond.

It gives peace and stillness to the soul
as it opens to the universe.

Because gratitude is a feeling and an
affirmation, there are no limits
to where it can expand.

There are no road blocks,
just an open path to wherever the heart,
soul and unlimited space take you.

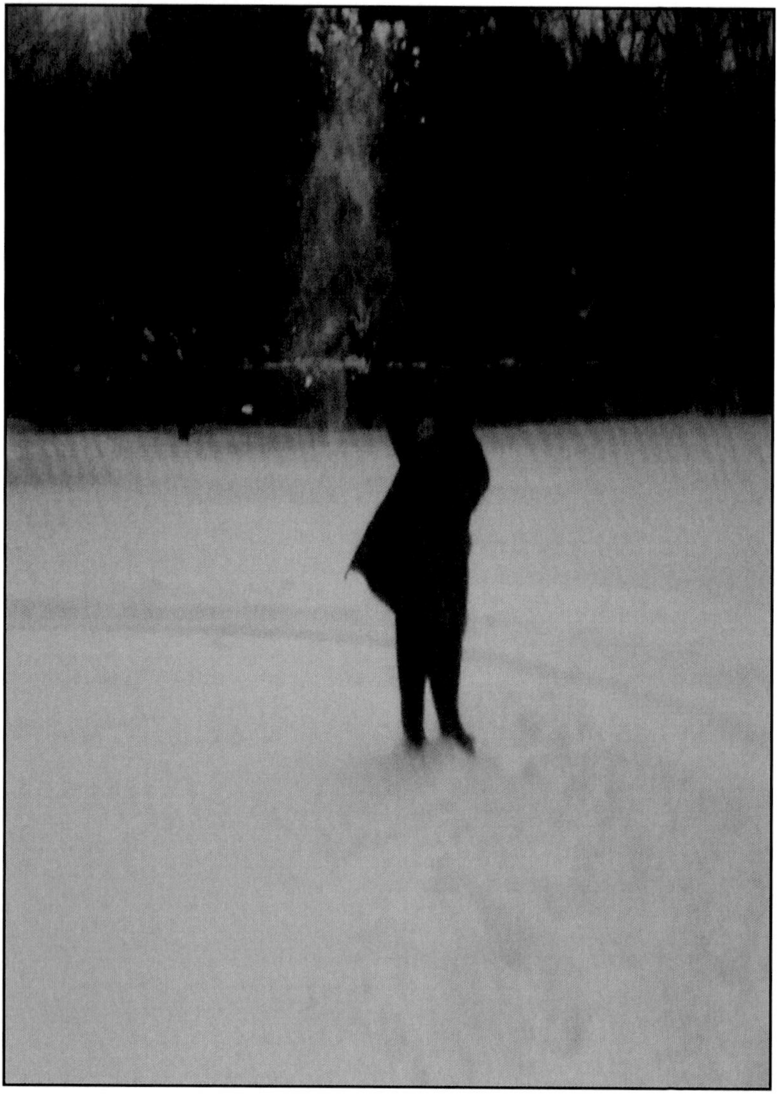

The purpose of the body is to house the soul.

That is the meaning of BEING.

To see that which exists without thought,

that is the formless.

This is the infinite spirit

that can coexist with

the form

and the mind.

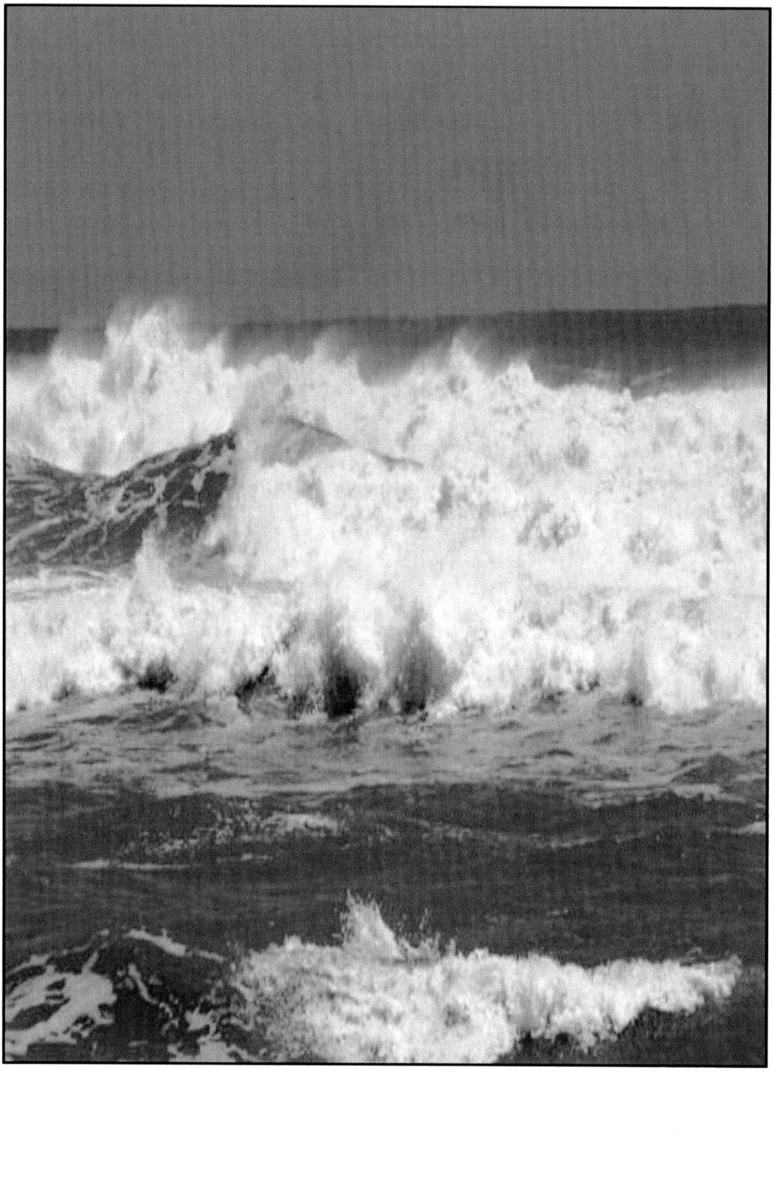

The ocean –
    mesmerizing,
        strong,
            massive:

As this powerful body of water approaches,
It gently embraces as it greets the shore.
And as I sit and watch, with slow breaths,
    I know I am One.

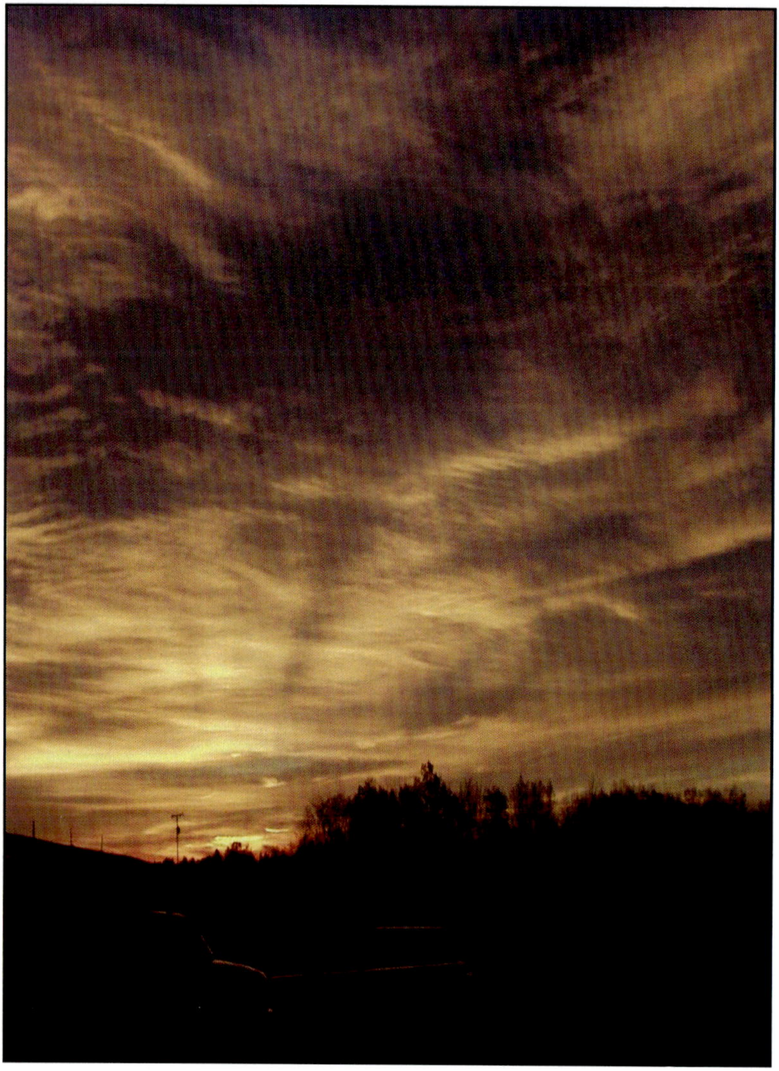

When the day motions to the night
to come forward
and the night becomes quiet and still,
that is when I,
with peace and contentment in my heart,
can find and reflect the moment.
And as the night begins
to merge once again with the day,
that is when I can reach beyond my being
and see the unseeable.
This is where I will meet you.

I have searched for a very long time
for the elusive answers to
life's universal questions.

As I drew closer to some of the
answers and was finally able
to hold them in my grasp,
I quickly learned that
universal knowledge
cannot be held in one's grasp.

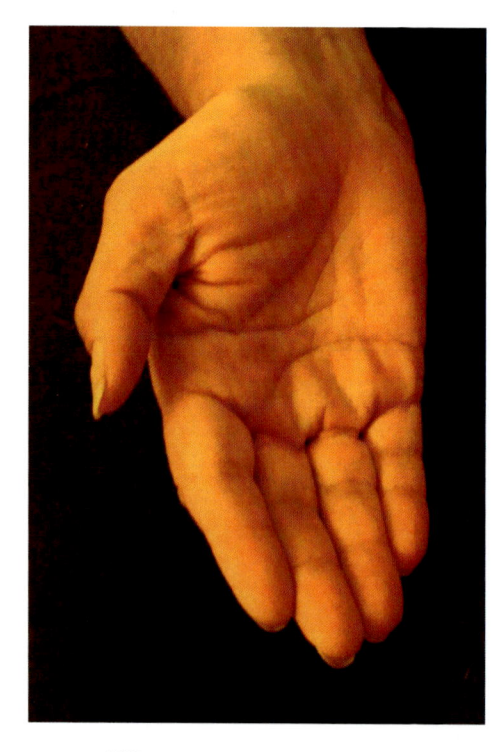

The hands are not large
or strong enough.
Nothing is large enough.

Knowledge is infinite,
and shall not be
contained within any boundaries.
What can be contained, is the
quest to obtain the unobtainable.

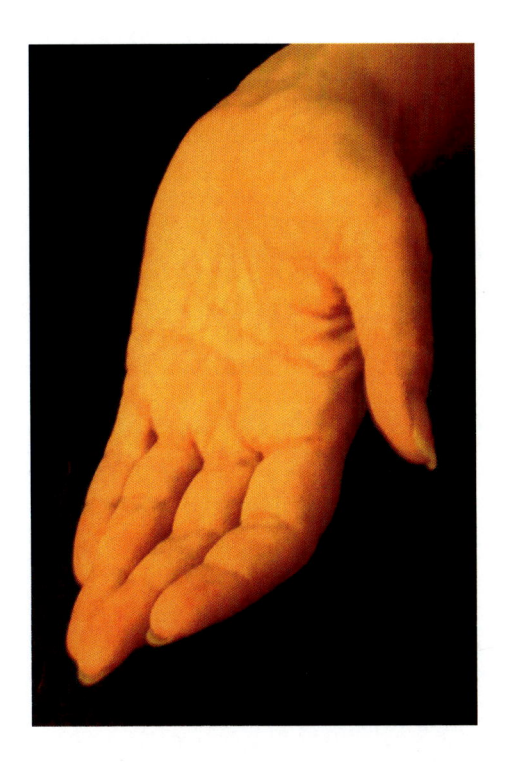

Daily

May your life be filled with continual
knowledge, insight and wisdom,
strength and compassion.

As we live we evolve, looking
introspectively, reflecting on our
feelings and thoughts, asking who
we are and what we want from this life.

Every motion ripples into another.

Every action creates another action,
which then creates another emotion
and each is one,
yet interconnected within the circle of life.

Affirmation

We are but reflections of ourselves
and each other.

I am an interconnected, interdependent
spirit, strong yet fragile.

I am where I have never been before
with myself and my relationships.

I trust in you and put myself in
your hands for safekeeping.

I thank you for all the fulfilling, gentle
yesterdays that you have given me,
and for all the tomorrows that you will bring.

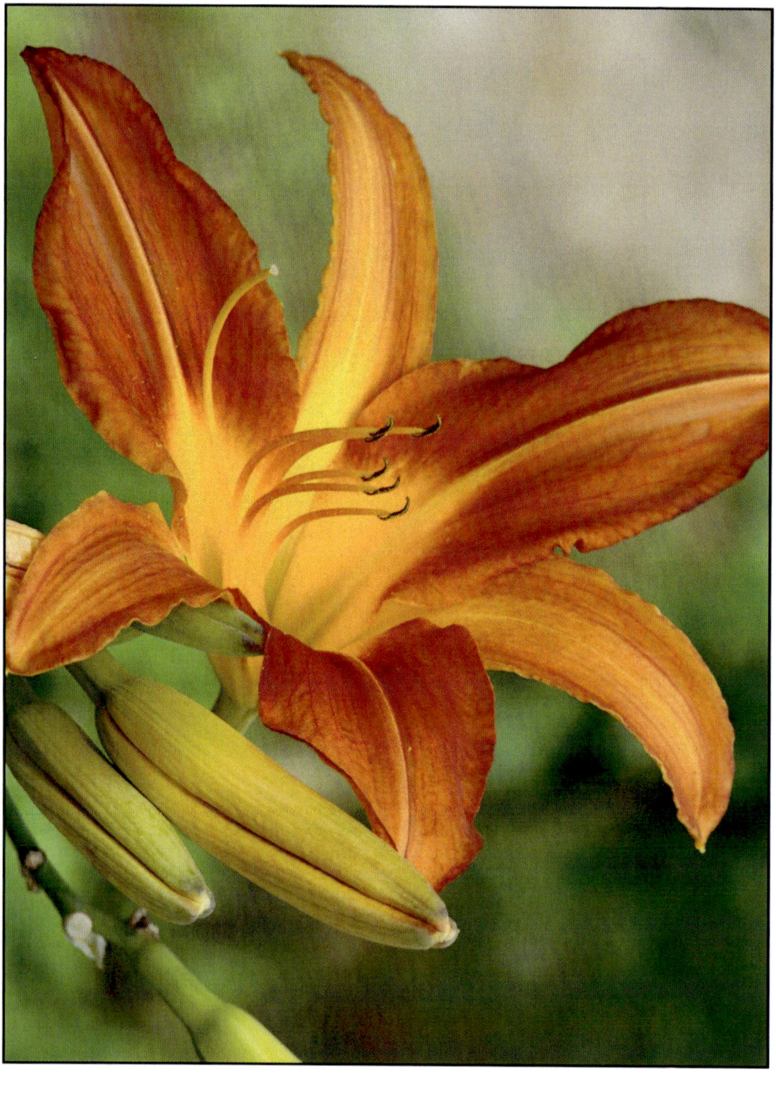

When one truly sees another's inner soul,
they see the universe.

Oneness, illumination, all that is near
creates a heavenly glow,
and the softness of light surrounds.

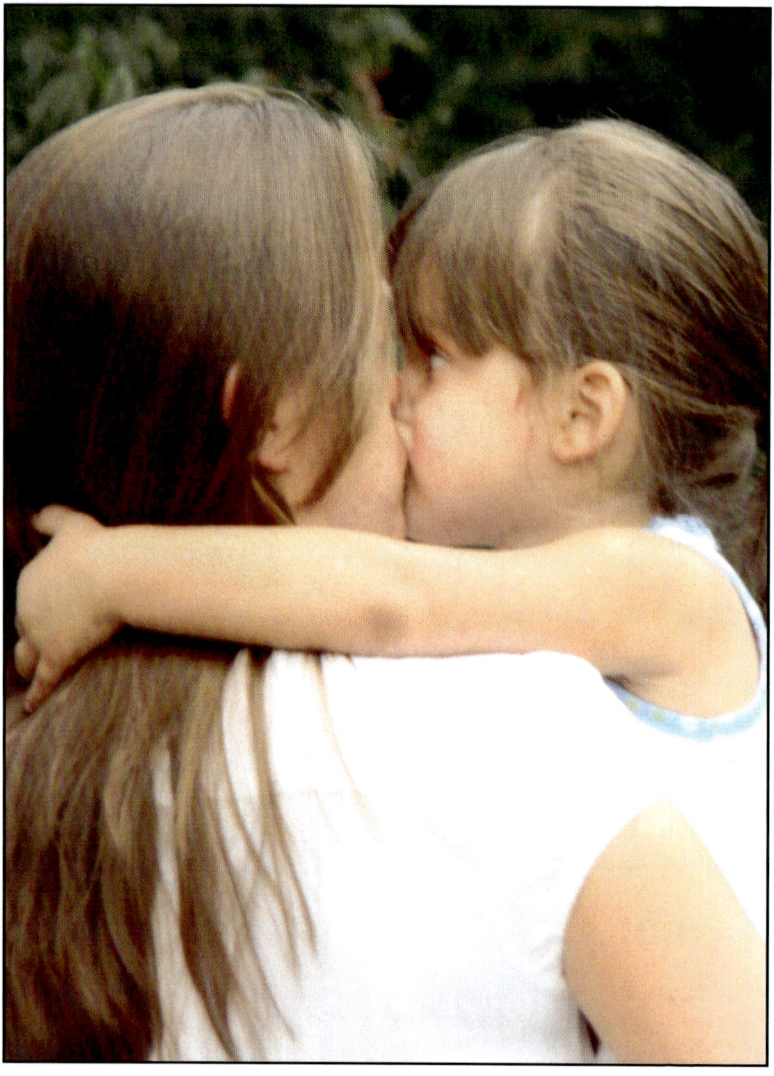

It is not a coincidence that human beings
connect, share, and give of one another,
interweaving their spirit and energy.

It is pure consciousness.

There is a reason and a purpose
created by life's forces and
omnipresent energies,
which present themselves to each other.

The sharing and giving
become an irreplaceable gift.

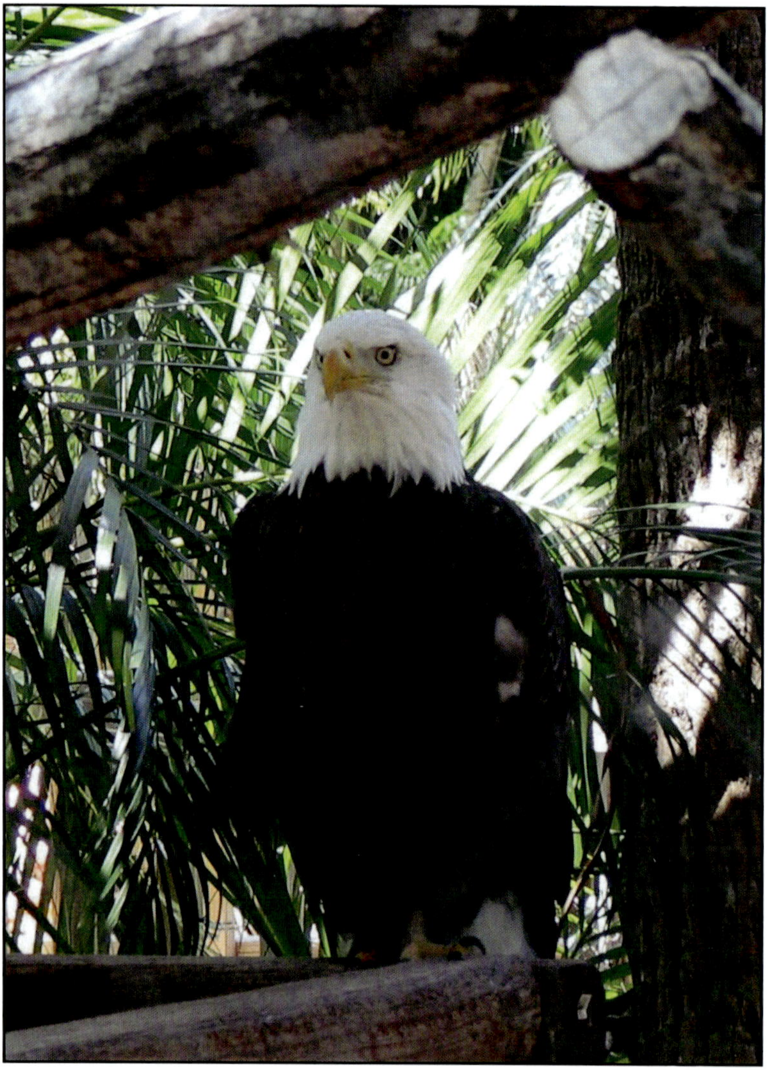

When those that you love are resting
and renewing their energy
in the arms of a greater spirit,
it is more than comforting.
It is a feeling of peace and trust.

To know the messenger
is to understand the message

The messenger is enveloped within
the message – they are one.

I will always keep open the message
while I hold the messenger deep
within my heart and soul,

For this is where all belief, knowledge,
and truth will be found.

The messenger reveals itself in many
beautiful ways--human forms,
spirits, guides and angels.

They all are the creation
from the greatest power.

As messengers
we are reflections of the universe.

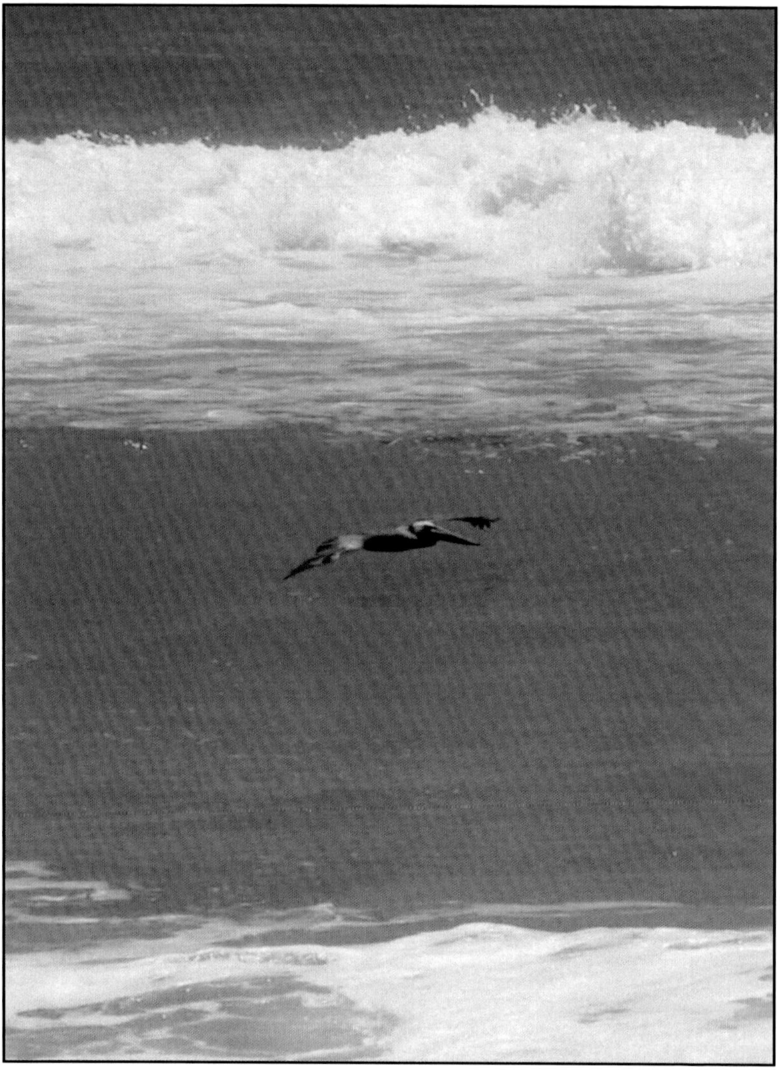

If I see a bird in flight and describe
only that here is a bird flying,
then I have separated myself
from that beauty of oneness which is
between the flight of the bird
and the universe.

In my thoughts and actions
I would have conveyed
only the bird.

I would have missed the
simplicity and at the same time
the complexity of the soaring flight.

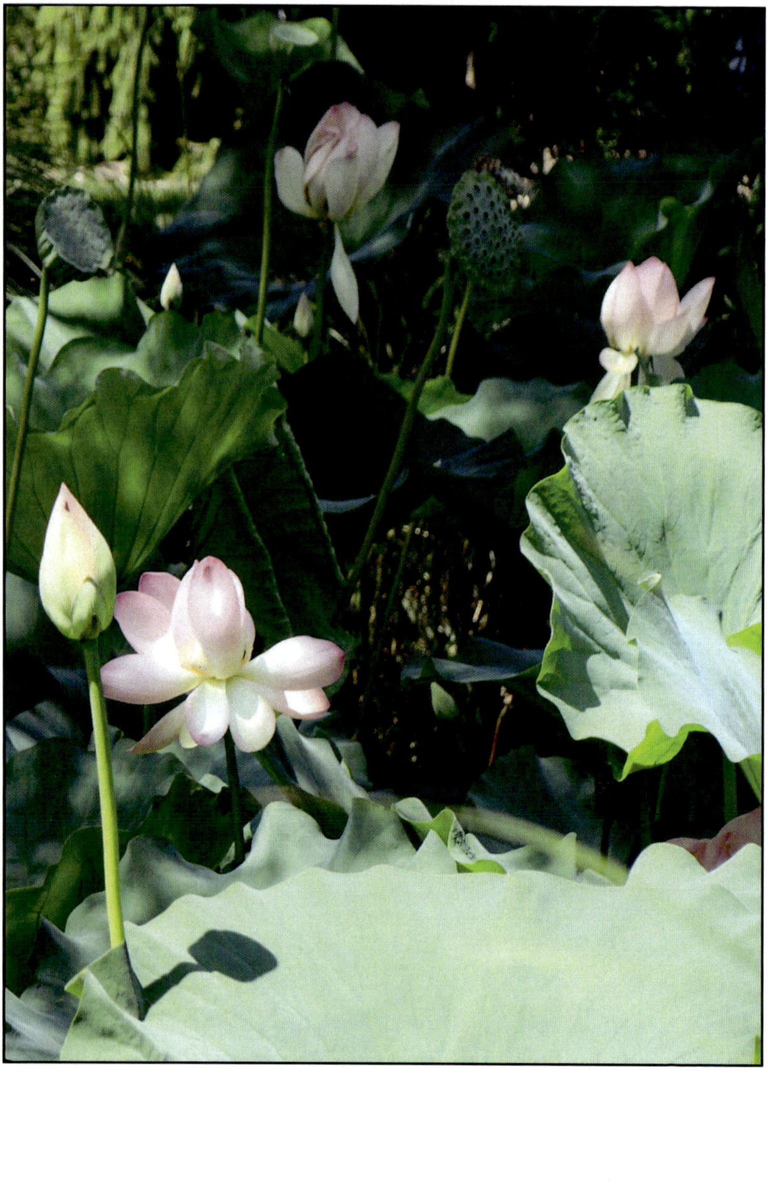

Through guiding energies, from the
extraordinary being that has shown me
today and tomorrow, I have evolved.
I have become a glowing light,
filled with love, understanding
and spirituality.

Reborn, I have opened myself up
like the lotus flower; its petals
outreaching daily, thirsting for energy
and knowledge, becoming enlightened.

Wherever the path takes me,
I will embrace it, for I know
that all is interconnected.

Additional Writings by Vicki Rickabaugh

Spirits United:
The Sacred Connection

With photography by
Pamela Turner

ISBN: 978-0-9829582-1-6

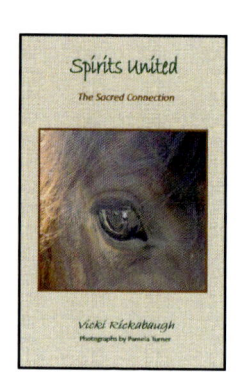

"I whisper in your ear, and you hear my dreams and aspirations. You sing to my heart whenever we are near. I sing back in refrain, our voices becoming one. My spirit will always dance with your spirit. Our spirits will always dance together. Once connected, we can never be apart."
Excerpt from Spirits United: The Sacred Connection

In the Beauty of the Sunset:
A Spiritual Journey

With photography by
Pamela Turner

ISBN: 978-0-9829582-3-0

"And when the winds blow so hard from every direction, so hard that I cannot stand any longer, I close my eyes and see your vision, know your strength, and believe."
Excerpt from In the Beauty of the Sunset: A Spiritual Journey

Published by Interwoven Connections
PO Box 686, Howell, NJ 07731
www.interwovenconnectionspubs.com